Take a
Chance on
Greece

BOOKS BY SUE ROBERTS

My Big Greek Summer

My Very Italian Holiday

You, Me and Italy

A Very French Affair

As Greek as It Gets

Some Like It Greek

Going Greek

Greece Actually

What Happens in Greece

SUE ROBERTS

Take a Chance on Greece

bookouture

Published by Bookouture in 2022

An imprint of Storyfire Ltd.
Carmelite House
50 Victoria Embankment
London EC4Y 0DZ

www.bookouture.com

ISBN: 978-1-80314-186-2
eBook ISBN: 978-1-80314-185-5

For Olivia and Frankie

PROLOGUE

I check into the most beautiful bedroom, with sheer blue curtains at the windows and brightly coloured art adorning the white walls. A vase of cornflowers, sitting in the middle of the windowsill in a white jug, look pretty and match the curtains either side. It's so fresh and welcoming and looks exactly like the brochure. Which makes a refreshing change.

Stepping out onto the small balcony, I catch my breath. I really hadn't expected a sea view and the sight of the sparkling water fills my heart with joy. A whole magical week here, before I move on. Exactly where to, I haven't quite decided yet, although I have a vague idea. For now, it just feels so good to be alive and I intend to savour every minute of my time here in Greece.

I'm taking in my surroundings, lost in thought when there's a tap on the bedroom door. It's the hotel owner, Sophia, brandishing a small kettle.

'I know how you English like your tea,' she says with a wink, setting the kettle and a handful of tea bags down onto a tray on the highly polished, dark wooden dressing table.

'Thank you, that's really kind.'

'*Parakalo*,' she replies, which I know means, you're welcome. 'There's camomile too, if you have trouble sleeping. Although not many people do, not with the sound of the sea to lull them to sleep. Enjoy your stay.'

When she breezes out of the room, leaving her floral scent in her wake, I grab a bottle of water from a small fridge and take it out onto the balcony, where there are two chairs and a table. I take a seat and stare out at the beautiful blue sea once more and give a sigh of pleasure. Something tells me I'm going to like it here.

ONE

There was a time when I never really understood why people suddenly had the desire to go travelling after receiving life-changing news. I mean, if you'd been through something terrible, wouldn't you want to be surrounded by the family and friends who had got you through it all, instead of wandering off somewhere in the distance?

Of course, that was before I received some earth-shattering news myself. Before I became ill, and everything changed.

My life seemed so small then, and I realised that there was a big world out there, ready to be discovered. I didn't want to die knowing I'd hardly done anything or been anywhere outside of the UK. I found this sudden desire to embrace life and everything that it had to offer. Life is for living, after all. Maybe that's what happens when you are staring death in the face. Or at least that's what I thought at the time...

Sitting at home recuperating, I think back to the day I was taken ill at work, on the sales order line for a shoe company. I remember trying to ignore the dull headache I'd had on and off for the past few weeks, preparing to head to the Greasy Spoon Café – which is actually a trendy café with stripped wooden tables and vegan alternatives for almost everything – with my good friend Polly for lunch. Polly ordered a bowl of vegetable soup, and I opted for cheese on toast and a pot of tea, a warming lunch for a cold day outside, the wind howling. I swallowed down two paracetamol tablets when Polly nipped to the toilet, as I didn't want this annoying headache to spoil our lunch together. I'd put them down to spending a lot of time in front of a computer screen, although my vision had been a little blurry of late as well, and I was considering maybe making an appointment with an optician to get my eyes tested.

Later that afternoon, Polly asked if I was okay, with a look of concern on her face.

'What? Yes, I'm okay. Why?' I replied, even though I'd begun to feel a little nauseous.

'It's just that you look a bit pasty,' she told me.

'Well, to tell you the truth, I do feel a bit off,' I admitted, taking a call for a shoe order.

'I've had a headache for a while now,' I continued, when I'd finished my call. 'But I just thought it was being sat at the computer for too long. And that cheese on toast has made me feel a bit queasy. I should have had the soup like you.'

'As long as you're okay... But honestly, you do look pale,' Polly said, looking really concerned now.

A short while later, I took a toilet break as nausea swept over me and my hands felt clammy. I went to the bathroom and splashed cold water over my face, before heading back to my desk, still feeling a little shaky. I assumed I'd picked up a virus, and was worried I might spread it.

As I walked along the corridor, I passed a row of half a dozen desks, the operators wearing headsets, all busy taking calls. Suddenly they seemed to double in number, as my eyes struggled to focus on the room in front of me.

'Orla, are you alright?' Janet, who was sat at the nearest desk, removed her headset and moved towards me and, as if in slow motion, her black skirt and pink blouse went fuzzy. Other people started to join her.

'Yes... I'm fine,' I muttered. 'I just feel a little...'

'There's a growth at the base of your skull but thankfully it's a benign mass. Try not to worry too much,' the doctor tells me gently.

I can hear the words coming out of the doctor's mouth, but I can't seem to take them in.

'A growth?' I say weakly.

'A meningioma, which is the most common type of primary brain tumour.'

'Brain tumour?' I can feel the colour drain from my face.

'I realise how alarming this must all sound,' the doctor continues. 'But thankfully it's not in a difficult place to locate. We can operate.'

As the doctor's words slowly sink in, I realise I will need surgery to remove the growth.

I'm sat in a grey-walled room with light-oak furniture as a neurosurgeon discusses the reasons for my recent headaches and blurred vision. Although I'm sat right here in front of him, it's as if he's talking to someone else. I almost turn around to see if someone is sat behind me, and I'm a voyeur in someone else's tragedy.

'Are you telling me I have a brain tumour?' I finally manage to gather my thoughts and ask the doctor.

I turn to look at my dad, feeling him squeeze my hand, and it's as if I've suddenly become aware that he's sat next to me. The first thing I think is how awful for him to be in this situation again. My mum passed from breast cancer two years ago and we both sat and listened to the doctor's prognosis in a room just like this on the floor above in this very hospital.

'Yes,' says the kind doctor, his face showing just the right

amount of concern and reassurance, making me think for a
second that I just might be okay. 'Thankfully it is a benign mass.
I realise how alarming it must be to receive such news, but the
scan shows that it's located in a place that means it's accessible
with surgery,' he says calmly. 'The survival rates for this type of
tumour really are very encouraging.'

'Right,' I mutter as tears threaten to fall as I finally take in
the news. A brain tumour? I'm struggling to process everything
I am being told.

The doctor has kind brown eyes and a confidence and calmness about him that I find reassuring.

'So, you say it's operable. Will you be doing my operation?' I
ask, trying to pull myself together.

'Yes, I'll be leading the team.' He smiles reassuringly.

'Sorry, Dad,' I say, hugging him tightly when the doctor
leaves.

'What on earth are you sorry for?'

My lovely, seventy-year-old dad gives me a squeeze.

'For putting you through this again.' I begin to cry.

'This is different,' he says positively. 'Didn't you hear that
surgeon. They've got it early. He said it's operable. I, for one,
believe him. He's a good man, he has a strong handshake.'

Heading to the car park, I climb into Dad's car as he drives
me to my old family home. I've packed only a few things as he's
insisted on me staying with him, so he can look after me.

'I hope I haven't interrupted your plans for today,' I tell him
as we drive. Since Mum's death, Dad has joined a golf club and
reignited his love of the game. Mum was poorly for two years,
outliving her prognosis of six months, and he spent his days
looking after her, as did I when work had finished. I feel almost
guilty that he wants to look after me, and I'm determined he
won't miss out on his social life and golf days.

I'm returning to hospital next week for my surgery, so spend
the time at Dad's, with him fussing over me and making me my

favourite childhood meal of fish fingers and beans for tea. Later, we do a jigsaw together, something I loved doing with him as a child. Although I lacked patience, he would always coax me and give me the confidence to complete it, praising me every time I slotted a piece into the picture.

I never really possessed much patience for many things when I was younger, flitting from job to job when I grew bored. Mum was disappointed when I dropped out of university in my second year, but Dad insisted I do what makes me happy, so I did. I tried every job you could think of, and when I was twenty-three, and bored of my job at the time, I actually ran away and joined the circus. Which wasn't quite as exciting as it might sound, as I worked selling tickets for the show and serving drinks and snacks in the big top. Even so, I travelled the length and breadth of England for a year, had a romance with a Russian acrobat called Pascha, and loved every single minute. I think Mum always thought I was 'a bit wild' and I would never settle down, but Dad told her not to worry and told me to spread my wings until a husband and kids came along – which, at thirty-two, still feels a long way off.

I find it so difficult to tell my friends at Potters, apart from Polly, of course, who is my absolute rock. She stays with me in my rented apartment for the odd night or two, when I'm in danger of falling apart in front of Dad, and I want to spare him and give us both some much-needed space. But, as the day of my operation grows closer, I feel calmer and more reassured, thoroughly googling brain tumours, and confirming everything the doctor told me.

The evening before my surgery, Polly calls around with a huge teddy bear from herself and my colleagues at Potters, along with some pyjamas, calming lavender bath goodies and a few other treats. The gift that stands out is a brand-new pink lipstick; it's so thoughtful, because my colleagues know that I'm never without my pink lipstick, that I have so many shades, from candyfloss pink to cerise. Today I'm wearing Raspberry Kiss. Even in my darkest times, I apply some lipstick; it's like my little piece of armour. With Dad out of the house and feeling the love from my workmates, a sudden fear grips me and the tears flow. And I sob until my ribs ache. Polly rocks me back and forth in her arms, telling me everything will be okay.

'But what if things go wrong? It's brain surgery. One slip of the knife and I'm done for. I'm not ready to die yet,' I blubber through the tears.

'It's obviously terrifying,' she tries to soothe me. 'But a doctor would never say your outlook was good if they thought otherwise, would they? I'm sure the surgeons have done this type of operation many times before.'

'I suppose so.' I sniff. 'I just hope everything goes well. You hear of things going wrong in surgery. It's the brain they're messing with, not a broken arm.'

'Things will not go wrong,' she says firmly. 'You'll be fine, and finally free of those headaches and the sickness you've been feeling, not to mention the problems with your vision. You'll be like a new woman.'

After we've chatted a bit longer, and Polly has calmed me down, as she usually does, she stands to leave.

'Good luck, we'll all be thinking about you tomorrow.'

My friend hugs me tightly at the front door before she leaves. 'And don't be skiving off for too long. I'll miss you. No one else likes going to the Greasy Spoon at lunchtime, they're still ordering from that delivery service that brings sandwiches to the office.'

She ruffles my hair, a tousled bob, currently dyed a silver-blonde colour that I think looks nice against my dark-grey eyes, and a lump forms in my throat.

'I might enjoy my cheese on toast a bit more next time we

go,' I say, thinking of how ill I was last time we visited and trying to be light-hearted. I don't want my friend worrying too much about me.

After Polly leaves, I read the comments in the card from my friends at Potters and I have to choke back tears again as they are full of so much love. I don't have many other friends, as I've changed jobs so often, I never really formed lasting friendships, and my college friends moved away a long time ago. But being at Potters for three whole years, it's like being part of one big happy family and I love them all.

Later that day, Dad returns from his golf game and makes me a hot chocolate before bed, just like he did when I was a little girl.

'Get some sleep, love, you need your rest. Big day tomorrow.'

'Thanks, Dad.' I smile, but my stomach is turning over with nerves. This time tomorrow evening I'll be sedated in a hospital bed, recovering from an operation I hope will be a complete success.

TWO

'There we go, love, extra vegetables for you, build you up a bit.'

It's six weeks after and I'm at Dad's facing a huge roast dinner.

'That looks amazing, Dad, but I'm not sure I can manage it all,' I say, eyeing the mound of roast beef, Yorkshire pudding and all the trimmings.

I know Dad is keen to look after me, but I can't wait to get out of here and go travelling. I have somewhere specific in mind. I need to see if I can find what you might call a missing piece of a jigsaw...

I suppose it was boredom, really, that had me looking for old photos of when I was a child. There was a box on the top of Dad's wardrobe, which had some cute photos and cards I'd made him for his birthday when I was a little girl. I remember sitting on his bed while he'd gone to the shops, smiling at some photos I had forgotten about, of a beach somewhere. It's also where I found the letter. When I heard Dad's key in the door, I quickly replaced the box where I'd found it once I'd written down the address of the sender.

'Well, do your best.' Dad smiles, bringing me back to the

present. 'Now that you're feeling a bit stronger, you won't mind if I go for a round of golf tomorrow morning, will you?'

'Of course not, Dad, you go and enjoy yourself.'

I'm grateful that he has been looking after me, but now that I'm recovering, I don't want him to put off his hobbies any longer. Besides, I can barely wait to go off on my travels.

I thank my lucky stars every single day that the operation was a complete success and I have been given a clean bill of health. I'm doing so well that I only have another week off work, then I'm supposed to be back at Potters. Although I'm looking forward to it in a way (especially catching up with my colleagues, given my brush with death), I also feel very restless. I had the most surreal dreams when I was sleeping in the hospital after my surgery; I've read accounts of people saying they have glimpsed white lights and what they believe to be heaven when they've been under anaesthetic, but perhaps it's our pre-conception of what we think heaven looks like. Personally, I dreamt of lush green landscapes, azure seas, and vast deserts. I saw polar ice caps and deep oceans filled with colourful marine life. I realised I was dreaming about Earth, the planet we inhabit right now, with all its wonderful diversity, and not some mystical utopia.

There are a couple of holiday brochures on the coffee table that I asked Dad to pick up from the travel agent in town and I happily browse them, dreaming of soft, sandy beaches and warm seas. It makes a nice change from binge watching Netflix series and playing Scrabble on my phone.

Perusing a Greek holiday brochure, my eyes fall upon the island of Kos, where we had the most wonderful childhood holidays when Mum was alive. The first time we went we hired a villa with my aunt, uncle and two cousins, but after that we always stayed at Villa Maria, a small hotel on the harbour front. If I close my eyes, I can still see the sparkling sea and the harbour where we took boat trips. On one of those trips, my cousin Martin – who was a little horror as a kid – snatched my sparkly flip-flops from my feet and threw them overboard, while Mum and Dad were fetching some drinks from a bar on the top deck. I got my revenge later in the holiday, though, when I hid his clothes in my backpack during a day out to a water park, and he had to walk back to the hotel draped in a towel. Happy days.

I don't want those childhood memories to be tainted after finding that letter of Dad's. They really were glorious times that I will treasure in my memory forever, and besides, I don't know the full story. All I do know is that I fell in love with Greece at a very early age.

I'm enjoying daydreaming about sunshine holidays, when there's a tap on the front door and I hear Dad inviting someone inside. It's Tim Potter sporting a huge bouquet of flowers.

'Oh, thanks, Tim. They're lovely.'

'From all of us at Potters. They all miss you, especially Polly.' He smiles.

'So, how are you then?' He sits opposite me on a floral-patterned armchair, whilst I'm on the matching sofa, surrounded by magazines and sweet wrappers. I kind of wish he'd told me he was coming as I might have tidied up a bit and maybe brushed some dry shampoo through my slightly greasy hair.

'Oh, you know, getting there. My memory is still a bit vague at times. Sorry, who did you say you were?'

Tim laughs loudly. 'Good one.'

'I'm doing fine. I'm getting bored actually, which means I must be on the mend.'

Tim tells me that the new range, providing larger size shoes and boots for drag artists, has gone down a storm. I'd already learned everything from Polly, of course, but I let him tell me all about it.

'I'm really pleased you went with the idea,' I tell him. I'd suggested it after taking a phone call from a bloke enquiring about size eleven sparkly boots. 'Potters must be one of the few manufacturers to offer such a service,' I say.

'Yeah, as Polly says, it's good to diversify a little. You can't afford to stand still in business, however well things are going.'

It's the second time Tim has brought Polly's name into the conversation, and I can't help noticing each time he mentions her a huge grin spreads across his face. Surely not?

Tim declines Dad's offer of jam roly-poly and custard – he's dressed smartly today in a blue crew neck jumper, smart jeans and trendy brown boots, so I guess he doesn't want to make a mess – but he does accept a cup of tea and a chocolate Hobnob. The snooker is on the telly in the background, and when Tim comments on the current players, Dad makes sure to let him know that there will never be anyone like Hurricane Higgins.

'Right, it's time I was getting on.' Tim stands to leave half an hour later, thanking Dad for the tea.

'See you at work soon then. And make sure you take regular breaks, ease yourself in gently.'

'Umm, great, thanks, Tim. I'm sure I'll be okay. And please thank everyone at work for the gifts. I've been truly spoilt.' I don't tell him that I'm unsure whether I will be staying on for too long when I return to work.

'You deserve it. Right, see you soon then. Thanks again,' he says to Dad, who walks him to the front door.

That evening when I settle down to sleep, I count my bless-ings once more. I've actually survived a brain tumour and I can't help wondering why. I'm a firm believer that everything happens for a reason. Maybe it's so I can look after Dad in his older years. I'm also financially secure thanks to my critical illness insurance payout. I've made a donation to a brain cancer charity, thinking of how others may not have been as lucky as I have been, and hoping that, one day, cancer will become a thing of the past. Or at least something that is curable in everyone.

With each day that passes, I have a renewed energy and a

desire to see some of the places I've dreamed about visiting all of my life. I've circled some of my favourite destinations and I'm hoping Polly might join me in some weekends away. After that I'm going to take a trip to Kos and feel the sunshine on my skin. And maybe pay a little visit to a place I hadn't been planning on visiting at all until a few weeks ago…

THREE

Much as I love my Potters family, I grow restless within a week of returning to work, as I imagined I would. There's a new starter called Patrick, who takes a bit of a shine to me and distracts me a little from my growing restlessness. We do actually go out on a date and have a nice time, and although he's handsome and caring, I don't think he's the one for me. This brief flirtation, while nice, gives me the last bit of impetus I need after my illness to get out and see this big, beautiful world. So off I go to explore some of our wonderful planet. Thankfully with the blessing of Tim, who kindly assured me that there would always be a job waiting for me when I returned from my travels, should I want it.

After travelling around Europe, I end up eating pastries in Paris, which I enjoy more than I ever thought possible, and even consider staying and signing up for a course in pastry making. I decide against it though, worrying that I might be overdoing things, so I return home. I've decided to put a Norwegian cruise on hold for now, although some day, I would love to see the Northern Lights.

One Sunday afternoon back in the UK, at a local pub

having a carvery with Dad, I ask him if he'd like to come to Greece with me. He thinks about it for a minute before declining the offer. Maybe deep down, I'm trying to gauge his reaction about returning to Kos.

'No, thanks, love, I'm alright here. I'm managing to get on with things. Kos might just bring too many memories to the surface.'

'Oh sorry, Dad, I never thought of that.'

And maybe some memories I knew nothing about, I can't help thinking.

'I thought you might just like some sunshine, but I understand,' I tell him. 'We haven't exactly had the best summer here.' I glance out of the window at a steady drizzle in late June.

'You go though,' Dad says. 'Enjoy yourself while you're young. I have a golf tournament coming up in a couple of weeks anyway. Just make sure you don't spend all of that insurance money though,' he advises me sensibly. 'You need to secure your future. The house isn't worth much,' he says, referring to the house I grew up in that he and Mum bought from the council.

Dad has always been good with money, so I take his point. I have spent quite a bit on travelling these past few months, that's true enough but there's still a large amount left. My critical insurance paid me over half a million pounds, which could go a long way in the North of England. And, of course, I can continue to work, should I ever need to.

'I know. And, to be honest, I've seen a lot of the places from my list. It's just a couple of weeks in Greece, relaxing and sunbathing. This will be a chill holiday, call it part of my recuperation. Tim has told me there will always be a job at Potters when I get home.'

Truthfully though, I'm not ready to settle anywhere right now. I want to grab life with both hands.

'That's good of him. And it will do you the world of good to get some sunshine on your skin and some healthy food,' Dad agrees.

'I might even act all grown up and actually buy a property,' I tell him, shocked at myself for actually saying this. I am thinking that I might buy somewhere, to rent out, but I don't reveal that part to Dad.

'Well, to be honest, it's probably about time you did. I'd like to see you all sorted before I depart this earth. I won't be around forever you know,' says Dad, perusing the dessert menu after his huge roast beef lunch.

'I think you're going to be around for a long time yet.' I smile. 'Don't you worry about that.'

FOUR

'I wish I was coming with you.'

Polly is sat across the table from me in the Greasy Spoon, where we've met for lunch.

'Why don't you?' I suggest as I stir my coffee.

'I've only got a week's holiday left, and by the sound of it you're going to be cruising around for a couple of weeks exploring. All that sunshine and Greek food.' She sighs.

'You could come over for a bit. Unless, of course, there's something, or should I say someone, far more interesting here.' I raise an eyebrow and Polly's cheeks flush red.

'What do you mean?'

'You and Tim. Is there something you're keeping quiet?'

Polly looks down into her coffee cup just as Sal, the café owner, places a serving of my favourite eggs Benedict down in front of me on the scrubbed wooden table, and a breakfast bap, filled with every breakfast item you can think of, in front of Polly. Everything is freshly griddled here and there's nothing greasy about it despite the name of the café.

I once asked Sal if she thought the title might put off young health-conscious diners, but she didn't think so. The café had been in the family for three generations and she had no intention of changing its name. 'And I wouldn't be too sure about those "health-conscious" youngsters. The place is packed out with them on a Sunday morning, craving a full English breakfast to cure their hangovers,' she said with a wink.

'I'm sorry I didn't say anything, I was going to, obviously, but it's early days,' says Polly, tucking a strand of her long red hair behind her ear.

'I can understand you not wanting to tell the others, but I'm your mate,' I say, slightly hurt that she hadn't confided in me. Maybe it's because she knows I once had a brief crush on Tim myself, but that was two years ago when I'd just split from a boyfriend.

'Well, I'm pleased for you. Tim's a good bloke. It's not as if there's anyone else at Potters.' I think of our line manager Mike and fifty-year-old Joe, both happily married for twenty years. There was the new guy, Patrick, but Polly's the kind of friend who wouldn't date someone I had, even if it wasn't serious. The rest of the staff are all female.

'I worked late one night a few weeks ago, helping with some admin work in the office when Megan was off sick. She's handed her notice in now, and Tim's offered me her job in the office.'

'Polly, that's great!'

'I'm still considering it,' she says, to my surprise. 'If me and Tim start openly dating, I don't want the others to think I've been promoted because I'm shagging the boss.'

'And are you?' I cheekily ask.

'No! We've only been out together twice, but you know what people are like. They probably don't realise I have worked in offices before.'

Polly worked in a timber yard before she came to Potters,

after the yard closed its business down. She told me her boss would sing 'Polly put the kettle on', which really grated on her nerves after a while.

Looking at Polly's pretty face and large green eyes, I think of handsome, dark-haired Tim. They would make a gorgeous couple. I really hope they make it official soon.

'Just one thing. How did you know about me and Tim?' she asks.

'Let's just say, he lit up at the mention of your name when he brought the flowers round,' I tell her, and she looks visibly chuffed.

'I hope you have the most wonderful time in Greece. I know how much you love the place. Send us lots of photos, won't you?' she says, reaching across the table and squeezing my hand. 'And don't be overdoing things.'

'I won't. And I'll be sure to send you lots of pictures. I think my wanderlust will be satisfied for a bit after this trip. I've ticked off a lot of places that were on my list. I now just want to lie on a beach and soak up a little culture in Greece.'

'You deserve it. You've been so brave. I'm not sure I could have coped as well as you did,' she tells me.

'You'd be surprised. You think you'll fall apart, yet somehow you develop this inner strength. I felt strangely calm before the surgery. Although I imagine everyone reacts differently.' I cut my knife into the eggs Benedict and savour a delicious mouthful.

After lunch, I head into Potters with Polly, where the gang surprise me with a chocolate cake, bearing the words 'Bon Voyage', and I'm almost reduced to tears once more. It feels so lovely being surrounded by the gang again.

Tim does a little speech, wishing me well and saying how

I've been missed during my absence, which is really lovely. Following the speech, the team hand over some more parcels, a travel mug and a map of Kos, as well as one hundred euros in an envelope.

'I have something for you all too.'

I place a gift on the table, and Tim invites Polly to open it.

'Ooh, thanks, Orla, we'll make short work of those biscuits. And, my goodness, we definitely needed some new mugs in the staffroom.'

The gang admire the pretty new set of bone china mugs and huge tin of assorted chocolate biscuits.

'You didn't have to do that,' says Tim. 'Portmeirion too, the good stuff.' He smiles. 'Very nice.'

'Too good for the likes of us,' says one of the sales people.

'Of course it isn't! And it's nothing really, compared to what you guys have done for me. I just wanted you all to know how much I appreciate you, and the support you have given me. You're the best.'

'Bring us back a jar of olives,' says Tim as they all wave me off from the car park and my heart swells with love for my Potters family.

I've been into town and had some pale pink streaks put through my silver-blonde hair and purchased a trendy cloche-style straw hat that was a real bargain at a vintage shop. I've packed lots of long, floaty dresses, vest tops and shorts and I'm ready to go.

'Make sure you ring me as soon as you arrive,' says Dad, hugging me as he drops me off at the airport.

'Of course I will. Take care, Dad. Remember I've prepared you a few nice meals in the freezer. Tomorrow's is already in the fridge, cheese and onion pie.'

Even though Dad's secret is weighing heavy on my mind,

he's still my father after all, and I want to make sure he eats properly in my absence.

'My favourite. I'll look forward to that. I might even have a slice later,' he says.

I'm collecting a car from the airport at Kos when I arrive, and I've booked myself into a small hotel from a bunch I'd looked at in the 'small and friendly' selection in the travel brochure. Normally, I'd just find something online through an Airbnb or similar, but I've discovered that, even though I'm back to good health, being ill has left me feeling a little vulnerable. I needed the security of a travel agent when I booked this journey. Despite that, I always feel safe wandering around Greece, especially Kos, and can hardly wait to go off exploring.

I feel a tingle of excitement when I board the plane and take my window seat. I love a window seat, as I enjoy watching the changing shapes of the clouds, and the feeling of flying like a bird through the sky as the little patches of green below get smaller, until we soar off to greater heights, finally floating above the clouds.

I'm glancing out of the window, watching the baggage handlers load the cases on board, when a male voice distracts me from my daydream.

'Hi.'

'Oh, hi. Sorry, I was miles away there.'

'You soon will be.' He smiles, drumming his fingers on the armrests. I notice his foot is twitching too.

'I take it you don't like flying then?' I say, seeing the telltale signs.

'Just the take-off. When's the bar open?' he jokes as he twists his expensive-looking watch around on his wrist.

He looks like a very well put together kind of guy, well

groomed and muscular, yet he's as nervous as a kitten. Just proves you can't judge a book by its cover.

'Sooner than you think. I'll hold your hand, if you like,' I say, wondering why on earth I just said that.

'You might need to,' he replies, with a genuine smile. At least he doesn't think he's sat next to a complete lunatic.

It's not long before the engines fire up and the familiar sound of engine thrust can be heard. I glance sideways at the guy, who has his eyes closed now, and seems to be saying a silent prayer.

A few minutes later we're airborne, and he is visibly relaxed.

'Phew. I'm glad that's over,' he says. 'I'm Dean by the way.' He's already eyeing the drinks trolley making its way down the aisle towards us.

He orders a vodka; I enjoy a small bottle of red wine and some Pringles.

'Where are you heading to?' he asks. 'I mean, I know you're heading to Kos obviously, but whereabouts?'

'Um, Kos Town,' I say, vaguely wondering if I ought to have told him that.

'Me too! Where are you staying?' he asks, becoming more mellow with every sip of his drink.

'With family. In a villa.' I'm not normally a cautious person but I don't know this bloke from Adam, so I don't want him knowing my exact location.

'Oh right.' Dean straightens up in his seat. 'Sounds nice, a villa. I'm staying in a cheap bed and breakfast. Had a bit of a tough year financially, if I'm honest,' he reveals. 'I used to own a bath and shower business; I had a showroom in town,' he tells me without me asking. 'But it closed down. Everyone buys online these days. It's killing the high street.'

'Sorry to hear that. What do you do now then?' I ask him.

'I sold off my stock, and set up an online business selling

beauty accessories including hair extensions. It was my daughter's idea.'

'The beauty business is definitely something that won't be going out of fashion anytime soon, I don't think. People like to look after themselves these days.'

'I know, and thankfully it seems to be taking off, fingers crossed,' he replies, giving me the name of the website. 'My daughter is only twenty, but she's brilliant. She's a graphic design student, she set up the website and everything. She's got a real business head on her.'

'Well, good luck with it all,' I tell him as I retrieve a book from my bag. I can't help thinking that he looks far too young to have a daughter of twenty, and wonder whether he may have had a little Botox, as he's clearly someone who likes to look after his appearance.

Dean is chatty and seems like a nice enough guy, so a short while later, when I need a break from reading, we strike up a conversation again. This time talk turns to various holiday destinations we've both visited, and I'm glad I have my recent trips to add to the discussion. An hour later, after another vodka, Dean falls fast asleep for a good part of the journey, so I return to my book. As we're coming into land, Dean fiddles with his watch strap once more, but we are soon on solid ground.

'Bye, then. Thanks for keeping me calm on the flight. Might see you around,' he says cheerfully as he heads off for a taxi, and I feel a bit mean thinking of him as a potential nuisance, but I guess you can't be too careful these days.

I check in with the smiling lady at the car rental desk, who leads me to the car park in blazing sunshine, the tall palm trees gently wafting in a light breeze. I'm wearing a long, sleeveless floral dress, and the hot sun caresses my bare arms as I walk. Once inside the car, I slip off my pink leather Doc Martens and replace them with a pair of denim flip-flops – they were made in Africa and the soles have been recycled from ACTUAL tyres, so they'll never wear out – before I give Dad a quick ring to let him know I've arrived safely.

When I've finished the call, I set the satnav and off I go, heading for the small hotel near the harbour in Kos. I can hardly wait!

FIVE

Heading along the harbour front, I recall the drive with Mum and Dad all those years ago. The anticipation we felt when we caught a glimpse of the sparkling blue sea, me excitedly asking if we could book a boat trip before we'd even arrived at our hotel.

Mum and Dad would smile and say, 'First things first', before unpacking at Villa Maria, the small hotel on the harbour front we returned to year after year. Maria became like an aunt in the end, fussing over me during our visits and when I was ten years old she taught me how to make hummus and tzatziki dips from scratch when I went through a no-meat phase.

After we'd unpacked, we would head to an ice-cream parlour where we would all enjoy a huge strawberry ice cream. Apart from Mum, who always insisted you couldn't beat vanilla, despite the array of flavours offered.

My parents were shocked to hear of Maria's untimely death, at the age of forty-five, and when we returned the following year her rather austere sister had taken over the hotel. Things were never really the same at Villa Maria, so we never returned. Dad thought it might be a fitting time to 'Try somewhere a bit different,' as we had holidayed in Kos for so many years. So, we visited Corfu, and Crete, further nurturing my love of the Greek islands, although Kos has always held a little piece of my heart.

Mum was visibly disappointed the first time I told her I didn't want to go on holiday with them.

'But you're only seventeen,' she said, ladling peas onto my plate, alongside a home-made steak pie.

'I'll be eighteen by the time the holiday comes around,' I reminded her.

My friends and I had booked a caravan for later that summer in Wales, when we would have all turned eighteen. A whole week away together for the first time, and we were all really looking forward to it. It turned out to be a disaster though as it rained for the whole week, and the caravan leaked. The onsite entertainment consisted of an old bloke in a three-piece suit and sparkly red bow tie singing Frank Sinatra tunes. The onsite pizza takeaway was closed for refurbishment and the disco was only on in the summer months – we went in September, just before the college term began. We would have known all of this had we read the information on the holiday park properly... But, somehow, we still managed to have fun, deciding that we would make the best of the situation. I like to think we brought a breath of fresh air to the pub the locals frequented in the nearby village.

'Mum, I'll never forgot our summer holidays, I have so many memories.' We were clearing the dishes away after dinner. 'And I'm so grateful you spent so long creating such lovely photo albums. But I'm really looking forward to having my very first holiday with some friends. It's time for you to go and enjoy some time with Dad now,' I remember telling her. 'You never know, it might turn into a second honeymoon.' I nudged her with my elbow and she coyly pushed a strand of her blonde hair behind her ear and laughed.

'What are you like? Although I suppose the Greek islands could bring out the romance in anyone,' she said with a faraway look in her eyes. 'Even your father.'

I've come to treasure those albums now, and Dad and I leaf through them from time to time, reminiscing.

I'm pulled out of my thoughts by the sight of Villa Sophia, which is set back from the main harbour, flanked by other guest houses and small hotels. It's painted a bright yellow, with dark window frames that make it stand out alongside its neighbouring apartments and hotels, which are mainly painted in white or soft pastel shades.

I park my car in the dusty car park at the rear of the property, with recycling bins in one corner, before I head inside to check in, just before noon.

'Then you don't need to bother coming back again. You think I am responsible for lizards on your balcony? You write a review like that, you make yourself look like a complete fool.'

A pretty woman, probably in her early fifties., with copper-coloured hair piled up on her head, slams the phone down at a wooden desk in the reception area. She's wearing red lipstick that matches her top and a pair of white trousers. She paints a smile on her face as she sees me.

'*Kalimera!*' she welcomes me warmly, surprising me by kissing me on both cheeks.

'Sorry about that. Would you believe I have a three-star review.' She waves three fingers furiously in front of me. 'Three. I always get five,' she huffs. 'I get three because they take a ground-floor room, and lizards like to play on their balcony. I tell them, this is Greece not Blackpool.' I laugh slightly nervously but, luckily, she quickly recovers her smile. 'Anyway, enough of that. Welcome to Sophia's hotel. I hope you will have a lovely holiday here in Kos.'

She clicks her fingers at a young man in a black T-shirt and jeans, who is hovering in a doorway on his mobile phone, before speaking to him in Greek.

'This is my son, Theo. He will show you to your room.'

Theo slides his phone into his pocket, and takes my heavy case before practically sprinting upstairs with it. He is undeniably handsome, but sullen and moody and looks like he would rather be anywhere else but here, in his mother's hotel in the height of the summer season.

I'm thrilled with the gorgeous room, blue, white and cool after the heat outside, and after a quick change into some shorts and a vest, I don my straw hat and head outside for a walk.

As I cross a road, a stretch of golden beach opens out before my eyes, the water beyond glistening in the sunshine. I climb down some beach steps and, after buying the traditional on arrival strawberry ice cream, I head to the water's edge and just stare out to sea. It feels so calming looking out across the waves, despite the beach being busy, and it makes me feel so small in the universe. Apart from my family and friends, would my absence in this world really have made a difference had I not been lucky enough to survive? Finishing my ice cream, I slip my sandals off and paddle in the warm sea, enjoying the feel of the water gently lapping across my feet.

I saunter across the sand, carrying my sandals, and watch the families enjoying their summer holidays, some enjoying picnics, others stretched out on sunloungers soaking up the rays. The sight of a father building sandcastles with his two young children, while his partner reads her book, transports me right back to my childhood when Dad would help me make the biggest sandcastle on the beach, with tall turrets and displaying the flags of different nations – that we'd collected over the years and always brought with us – as Mum read her book. Sometimes, I wish those days could have lasted forever. I thought we had all been so happy then, but I guess I was seeing everything through a child's eyes.

Heading to a beach bar, I spot Sophia's son, Theo, sitting on a bar stool chatting to a guy behind the bar. He turns and smiles as I take a seat at one of the tables after ordering a beer. To my surprise, when my drink arrives, he finishes his conversation with the barman, and strolls over to join me.

'Are you having a nice day?' he asks, regarding me with his dark-brown eyes, the same colour as his hair that is lightly streaked with gold.

'Lovely, thanks. The weather here makes a glorious change from the North of England.'

'Have you been to Kos before?' he asks.

'Not since I was a kid.' I take a sip of the golden, ice-cold beer. 'But I have the fondest memories. It hasn't really changed much. From what I can remember, that is.'

I tell him how we used to stay at a hotel further down the coast road.

'I picked your place from a selection of small and friendly places. It sounded just perfect.'

'To a visitor, I suppose it is. My mother is proud of the hotel's reputation, although she works me into the ground.' He pulls a face.

'Yep. You look really stressed, sitting with a cold drink chatting in a beach bar, the sound of the sea in the background.'

He smiles as he glances at his watch.

'Right, I must be leaving as I have to collect someone from the airport. Although, yes, I guess there are worse ways to make a living. Enjoy your holiday, no doubt I will see you later,' he says, before draining his glass of Coke and heading off.

'Now that is someone I don't mind watching leave. Just look at that backside.'

A slim, stylishly dressed Englishwoman has slid into an empty seat opposite and appears to be speaking to me as she watches Theo head off over a zebra crossing. She lowers her sunglasses down to get a better view.

I can't help wondering whether or not she meant to say the words out loud.

'Oh gosh? Did I actually say that? Sorry.' She laughs, breaking into my thoughts. She introduces herself as Rose, extending her perfectly manicured hand for me to shake. 'I do know the owner of the glorious backside though; his name is Theo.'

'Yes, I'm staying at his family hotel,' I tell her and introduce myself.

'Orla, that's a nice name. It's Irish, right?'

'Yes. I'm named after my grandmother,' I tell her.

Funnily enough, I hated my name when I was young, wishing I could be called something like Joanne or Kelly, like my other friends. I've grown to love it though, as it's a little more unusual, in England at least.

'Anyway, I think it's the hormone replacement therapy.' She lights up a cigarette, after asking if I mind.

'What is?' I ask, confused.

She's wearing a white scarf rather than a sun hat, à la Audrey Hepburn, and designer sunglasses, perched on top of her head. She has striking pale-blue eyes and is wearing a slash of red lipstick on her lips.

'My reignited libido. I've gone a little sex mad,' she reveals, giving the throaty laugh of someone who probably smokes too many cigarettes. 'Which is ironic really,' she continues. 'My husband divorced me, as I had gone off sex and he hadn't, so he went elsewhere.' She blows a line of smoke sideways, away from me, towards an empty table. 'Now I just want to jump into bed with every good-looking man I meet.'

'How lovely,' I reply, which seems like a completely inappropriate response.

'Oh no, it isn't lovely.' She shakes her head. 'I have an appointment with my GP to change my hormone replacement medication. I can't go on like this. I don't indulge my desires, of course. Well, maybe I have once or twice, but it is rather frustrating feeling this way all the time.' She sighs. 'So, I came here to practise some yoga, go swimming and try and relax after the stress of the divorce.'

She tells me about her morning yoga class that starts at six thirty in the morning on the beach.

'Just over there.' She points to a stretch of sand further down the beach, near an upturned fishing boat. 'Hosted by none other than our lovely Theo.'

'Theo's a yoga instructor? Really?'

'It would appear he is a man of many talents,' she says, giving a slow smile.

'I might just do that. Yoga on the beach sounds wonderful.'

'Oh, it really is. It's nothing like the yoga I used to do back home in a freezing cold community centre.' She laughs.

'I know what you mean,' I say. I used to enjoy the occasional yoga session but hadn't been to classes after I developed the headaches and blurred vision.

'So, what's your story? Actually, do you fancy a cocktail?' Rose asks, and before I have a chance to answer, she's called a waiter over.

'Um, okay sure, I am on holiday after all. I think I'll have a mojito.'

'Lovely, make that two.' Rose takes a compact from her bag and reapplies her red lipstick.

When I've finished telling her my story, she leans back in her chair.

'Wow. I did not expect you to say that. I imagined you were travelling with friends, which I realise is a very sweeping generalisation. Lots of women travel alone nowadays, as do I. Are you alright now?' she asks, frowning slightly.

'Yes, I feel wonderful. The surgery was completely successful, thank goodness.'

'Are you alright in this heat?' She looks a little doubtful.

'Fine. I adore the hot weather, I always have.'

I have skin that tans easily, and my natural hair colour is probably between a dark blonde to a mid brown.

'Well, make sure you drink plenty of water,' she advises.

'I know. I will.' I nod.

'Of course you know! What am I like, sorry. Ah, to be your age again.'

Our mojitos have arrived and she takes a long sip. 'The younger generation have so much more courage these days. My twenty-two-year-old neighbour took off to Thailand on her own last year. Alone! No such thing happened when I was young, my mother would have died of a heart attack at the very thought.' She laughs the throaty laugh once more.

She's a very attractive woman, who could be anything from mid-forties, to mid-fifties. Her skin is unlined and she has clearly spent a lot of time, and possibly money, looking after herself, although it seems you can't trick nature who will send the menopause when it's good and ready.

I sip the last of my delicious mojito, enjoying Rose's company, when a group of muscled blokes in shorts embark on a beach volleyball game close by, and Rose looks as if she might spontaneously combust. She takes a fan from her bag and waves it furiously in front of her face.

'Right, I'm off to have a cold shower. It's suddenly become very hot around here. Enjoy the rest of your day, Orla. Maybe I'll see you in the morning at yoga.'

'Maybe you will. Bye, Rose. It was good to meet you.'

'You too.' She smiles, and then she's gone.

SIX

I spend another hour at the beach bar, sipping cold drinks and people-watching beneath the shade of the straw roof. Jet-skiers zip along the water and small boats are chugging back into the harbour after a trip out to sea, evoking childhood memories once more. Dad would hire a speedboat and take us out for the afternoon when I was little, although when the water got a little rough, and the boat would bounce along the waves, I would feel incredibly sick.

A bloke at the next table catches my eye and asks if he can join me. I must either have a very friendly face, or this is what happens when a woman is sat at a beach bar alone. But he's very handsome, and it can't do any harm.

'I'm Jack,' he says, taking the chair opposite me.

'Orla, nice to meet you.'

Jack's probably around my age, with blonde hair and tanned skin. I don't know how he can't be roasting in his black T-shirt and denim shorts.

'Are you here on holiday?' he asks, taking a sip of his beer.

'I am. How about you?'

I'm wondering whether I ought to mention the family villa

again. But then, I am staying in a very public place, with a hotel owner who would surely stand no nonsense from unwelcome visitors.

'I live here now.' He takes another sip of his beer. 'I made the move four years ago. Couldn't get enough of the place when I came on holiday, so I decided to move out here permanently, before I had any commitments.'

'Where's home?' I ask, unable to place his accent.

'Leeds. Although I lived in Manchester for ten years as a kid, then Essex. We moved around a lot with my dad's job.'

'I can understand the appeal in living here. I holidayed here for years as a kid too. How do you earn a living out here?' I ask, sipping the last of my mineral water.

'I run boat trips. Off duty I'm just Jack, but when I'm working I'm Captain Jack Sparrow on the pirate ship the *Treasure Chest*.' He adopts a pirate accent.

So maybe he's just trying to flog me a boat trip.

'Didn't Jack Sparrow captain the *Black Pearl*?'

'He did. I just didn't want to risk a lawsuit over copyright, especially calling myself Jack Sparrow.' He laughs.

I recall seeing the pirate boat down at the harbour, towering over the other boats.

'That sounds like a lot of fun,' I say, waiting for his sales pitch, but there isn't one.

'The kids love it. And the adults too, especially after a couple of drinks. We have sword fights along to the *Pirates of the Caribbean* soundtrack.'

'I can imagine that. I bet it's a popular trip.'

'It is thankfully. The kids love it when we pretend to make their parents walk the plank for not letting them stay up late, or whatever they tell us. One guy was a bit pissed last week though and we nearly lost him overboard for real.' He laughs again.

'Oh my goodness!' I can't help giggling.

'I know. I can laugh about it now, but I'd be closed down

right away if there was an accident. We offer strictly two small beers included in the price, but he'd obviously been drinking before. Or sneaked something on board.'

'A bottle of rum, maybe?'

'Ha. Maybe.'

He finishes his drink and makes to head off.

'Well, enjoy your holiday, Orla. You can't miss the pirate boat, it's halfway along the harbour. Come say hi, if you're passing. Don't worry, I won't try and flog you a trip. Unless you fancy one, of course.'

He runs his hand through his tousled blonde hair, his smile revealing perfect white teeth, and then he disappears. People are so friendly here, I'm wondering who might come along next and strike up a conversation. I debate staying a while longer, staring out over the water as the sun begins to drop, but think I'll head along the strip of restaurants across the road and stake out somewhere for dinner later.

SEVEN

There are so many restaurants, offering platters of delicious seafood, mixed mezes and barbequed meats. I'm spoiled for choice, as every eatery, packed in next to each other all down the length of the strip, looks and smells so enticing. Neon lights flash from café signs selling snacks and beers and chalkboard specials are written up outside many of the tempting cafés. Among the traditional Greek tavernas, there are one or two Italian and Chinese restaurants, as well as places offering pancakes and delicious chicken gyros, the meat slowly rotating on spits outside each café.

I'm glancing at a menu chalked on a board in the shape of a fish outside an attractive-looking restaurant, and as I turn to walk on, not really looking where I'm going, I crash into someone.

'Oh, I'm so sorry.' I look into the dark eyes of a handsome Greek guy of around my own age, who looks mildly irritated. I'm sure I hear him tut.

'It's okay,' he says, his face unsmiling as he enters the same restaurant I was investigating, leaving a whiff of expensive after-shave in his wake.

Maybe I will eat here tonight; the smell from inside is so enticing it makes my mouth water. And if the Greek guy is eating here now, hopefully I won't run into him again later.

Heading away from the restaurants, I walk towards the castle, along the promenade known as the Avenue of the Palms, for the huge trees that tower over the water, gently waving in the sea breeze. I take in the sights, stopping at the Tree of Hippocrates, surrounded by a fence. I remember Dad explaining the Hippocratic oath to me, which all doctors take to this very day, and how Kos is the birthplace of Hippocrates himself.

I walk alongside the stunning castle and head through a stone archway. There are beautiful, vibrant flowers along the sides of the castle, as well as cycle paths, busy with people taking bike rides while enjoying the beautiful weather. Walking on, I pass some little shrines at the roadside that look like minia-ture churches, painted white with a blue roof with a cross on the top. Inside, there are framed photos of loved ones, some with small gifts of flowers. It's such a lovely idea and I find myself wondering why we don't do something similar back home in England.

A while later, I make my way back to the hotel, the little blue tourist train passing me by with a toot toot as tourists sit aboard, smiling with giggling children. I remember taking this train as a young child, and how happy I felt when we stepped aboard. Dad would always tell me we were going on a mystery tour when I asked him where we were heading. I found the idea of a mystery tour so thrilling.

'Just in time,' Sophia greets me as I return to the villa. She leads me through the lounge into a large rear garden, where a long table has been set under a gazebo. There are squares of baklava, scones and lemon cake, along with jugs of iced peach tea. Several other residents are sat around the table, including an American couple, and two English girls, who look to be in their mid-twenties.

'I'd forgotten all about the tea at three,' I tell Sophia after introductions are made. 'I thought this was more of a British tradition.' I sink my teeth into a sticky piece of baklava, rich with figs and nuts.

'I suppose it is. But in my experience, no one turns down cake if it is offered. Besides, I do have a lot of English guests. Oh, and I like my guests to get to know one another. Friday evening is BBQ evening if you are interested. Twelve euros including drinks.'

'That sounds lovely, thanks.' An evening BBQ sounds like a great way to get to know all of the guests. I'm really looking forward to finding out more about them.

Despite the heat of the day, Sophia still looks as cool as a cucumber while she attends to her guests.

'Oh my gosh, this lemon cake is just gorgeous,' says one of the young women, wearing tiny white shorts and a yellow vest top. Her friend is as blonde as she is dark, hair styled long and straight. The two are dressed similarly but the friend's shorts are denim and her T-shirt white.

'You're right, who can resist a bit of cake. Although, we'll have to pass on the BBQ. We'll be hitting the bars in Tigaki on Friday night, if anyone fancies joining us?' The blonde girl seems to direct this comment at me, being the only one of a similar age I suppose. 'I'm Chloe by the way, and this is Amy, or Ames as I call her,' she says in her unmistakeable Liverpool accent.

'We're not too old to party, you know,' says Brady in a broad southern drawl. 'Although, I must say I love nothing better than a darn good BBQ.' He chuckles and his blue and white shirt struggles to contain his sprawling tummy. Iris, his attractive wife, pats her strawberry-blonde hair and crosses her tanned, slim legs. 'You speak for yourself, Brady. I just might dig out those dancing shoes and join you girls.' She winks and I smile as I imagine her ripping up the dance floor, giving the young ones a run for their money.

We sit around drinking peach tea and getting to know each other in the shade of the gazebo, working on polishing off the last of the cake. By the end of the afternoon, everyone is in good spirits and looking forward to the BBQ on Friday evening.

'Oh, and there will be Greek dancing around the pool at the BBQ evening. Joining in is not compulsory, but expected,' says Sophia with a wink, before she wafts off.

Amy and Chloe decide to lounge around the pool on sunbeds as the Americans head upstairs for a siesta, feeling tired after their long flight from Texas.

'So, is that everyone who is staying here?' I ask Sophia as she clears the table after the afternoon tea. I know there are only four bedrooms, two downstairs and two on the first floor. Both the upstairs rooms, mine and the one next door to me, have balconies to allow guests to enjoy the view and the sun in private.

'Almost everyone. We have someone in the room next to you, who obviously prefers his own company. Theo collected him from the airport earlier. But, of course, that is fine. People want different things from a holiday.' She smiles brightly.

After changing into my swimwear, I settle down on a sunbed by the swimming pool and feel my eyelids close as my body gives in to the soothing effects of the hot sun. An hour later, I wake and reapply sun lotion, feeling the burn on my skin and a slightly tight feeling in my face. Oh bugger. I'm probably going to have a bright red face right now and can't believe I fell asleep without covering myself with a parasol first.

A little while later, I prise myself from my sunbed and head upstairs for a cooling shower before I go out for an evening meal in town. Sunset is one of my favourite times of the day, when the sun begins to dip and the lights come on in the bars and restaurants, giving everything a magical, holiday feel.

Chloe and Amy are sat on bar stools, sipping cocktails at the tiny bar near the pool, as I head to my room.

'Bye, hun,' says Chloe as I walk past. 'If you fancy a dance later we'll be at Mambo's around nine o'clock. It's at the other end of the harbour, across the road from the pirate ship.'

'Great, thanks, maybe I'll see you there.'

Heading upstairs to my bedroom, the bloke staying next door to me is fumbling with his door key.

'Hi,' I say cheerfully.

'Hello.' He turns to look at me, barely raising a smile, and I recognise him at once. It's the guy I bumped into outside the fish restaurant.

I open my mouth to say something else, but he steps inside his room and closes the door.

'Pleased to meet you too,' I mutter to myself.

The streets are buzzing as I head along to the restaurant I chose earlier today. Families are walking along, with children licking ice creams and carrying glow in the dark toys from the stands that line the strip. There's a lovely holiday vibe here, as laughter blends into the sound of music belting out from one of the bars and loved-up couples walk hand in hand along the road, with the sea lapping on the sand on the beach opposite.

An orange sun seems to hover in an almost lilac-streaked sky and as I cross the road, I see the wooden pirate boat making its way back towards the harbour. I imagine Jack brandishing his sword and entertaining the children on board with tales of pirate skulduggery and smile to myself. Walking on, the smell from a stand selling chicken gyros makes my stomach rumble a little in anticipation of my evening meal. I'm glad I only ate a couple of small pieces of cake earlier, as it's eight o'clock now and I want to make the most of the wonderful food on offer.

Soon enough, the blue-painted restaurant comes into view, its menu displayed on the large fish-shaped blackboard outside. The ground level is a bar area filled with people enjoying beers or pre-dinner cocktails. A waiter leads me down a slope to the restaurant area, which surprises me with its quirky decorations. Wooden tree trunks, serving as coffee tables, have old-fashioned telephones on them in various colours. Toy monkeys and lemurs hang from trees strung with coloured lights. There's even a red English phone box in one corner. The tables all have brightly coloured mismatched chairs and are covered in paper tablecloths, each with a huge map of the island. The smell is so tantalising and, glancing around, I can see that the portions being delivered to tables are huge.

Once I'm seated, the waitress hands me a menu and tells me that rabbit stew is the speciality of the day, cooked slowly in red wine and onions. I thank her, but pass on that – I had two as pets when I was a child, so I could never ever bring myself to eat rabbit. I order a carafe of white wine, before ordering the stuffed sea bass that I'd already decided on when looking at the menu this afternoon.

'What's with the phone box?' I ask the waitress who returns with my wine.

'It was a gift, 'she tells me. 'My grandparents own this restaurant and love unusual things. My grandfather had an English friend who lived here for many years and had it in his garden. He dined here all the time apparently. When his friend passed away, his widow gifted it to my grandfather. He says it is a perfect reminder of his friend. Although, I believe his wife never did like it in her garden.' She laughs.

'I must say, it does fit in well with the restaurant, given its quirky style, if that's the right word.'

'I think that is exactly the right word,' she says, before she heads to the kitchen with my food order.

I take a sip of my cold, crisp wine and glance around at the other diners in the restaurant: a mixture of families and couples, as well as one or two lone diners like myself. A pretty woman with her dark hair in a layered bob glances at her watch before spearing an olive with a cocktail stick. She takes a long glug of her red wine, before her date eventually arrives.

'I'm so sorry.' He holds his hand up. 'I decided to drive into Kefalos earlier. There was some sort of street parade and I got stuck in traffic,' he explains as he sits down.

'You seem to be having a lot of trouble with your timing.' She takes a sip of her wine. 'I hope you're not going to be asking for an extension on your book; we have a production schedule to stick to.'

I'm stunned to discover it's the guy from the room next door to mine at the hotel. So, he's a writer?

'Of course not. You'll have the first draft in three weeks just as I promised.' I'm sure she notices his jaw twitch slightly.

'So how are you getting on with it? Has being here inspired you, as you hoped it would?' she asks.

'Yes, it was the right thing to do, I'm certain of it. The story is flowing well since I have been here.'

'Well, I'm pleased to hear it.'

She pours him a glass of wine from a bottle and he takes a sip.

'I can see why you feel inspired here,' says the dark-haired lady. 'I'm only here for a few days, attending a wedding, but wish I was here longer. I'm glad the first draft will be with me on time.' She smiles.

'It definitely will.' He returns the smile, but it looks somewhat strained. Changing the subject, he continues, 'I recommend the lamb with dauphinoise potatoes, it's quite something.'

'Sounds good.'

He glances around in search of a waiter and as he catches my eye I wave. He gives me a curt nod before returning his attention to the woman in front of him. He's very handsome in profile, dark eyes and hair, the slight curl to it accentuating his strong jawline. There's, annoyingly, something quite captivating about him.

A few minutes later, my waitress appears at his table and, to my surprise, she greets him with a hug. Maybe she's his girlfriend.

I tuck into my delicious sea bass stuffed with tomatoes, garlic and fennel, alongside a dish of wonderful roasted potatoes and green beans tossed in lemon, and forget all about my hotel neighbour as I devour every delicious mouthful.

Around an hour later, finishing with a creamy cappuccino, I pay the bill and head off. My neighbour appears to be wrapping up his meeting at the same time and also stands to leave.

This time, I decide not to make eye contact with him, but as I move to walk on, I suddenly hear a voice behind me.

'Sorry if I've appeared a little off,' he says as I turn. He's wearing dark denim jeans and a tight-fitting, white T-shirt that hugs his body in all the right places, and a leather necklace around his neck. 'I'm Georgios.' I can't help noticing he has a British accent, despite looking Greek.

'I'm Orla. And it's okay.' I shrug. 'I guess we all have our off days.'

'It's not exactly an off day. I'm just a little under pressure,' he replies, a little curtly.

'We live in a stressful world.' I smile at him, but he doesn't return it.

'I just need to be left alone at the moment, to get on with my work.'

'Right, bye then.' I make to walk off, expecting him to laugh. He doesn't. Wow, this guy is hard work.

'Right, okay. See you around I expect,' he says, and then he's gone.

I head off, pondering the brief encounter with the clearly stressed, but undoubtedly handsome, resident of the hotel for a bit, before putting it out of my mind as I take in the sights and sounds of the busy harbour front. Children's excited squeals from the rides of a small funfair and the aroma of pancakes being freshly made on a stall waft towards me on the air as I stroll by. I pass a little outdoor market, vendors selling everything from pretty silver jewellery to touristy key rings and mugs with the word Kos and the Greek flag emblazoned across them. Several customers are huddled around a stall, trying free samples of honey and ouzo.

I cut down a side street across the road from the pirate boat and find myself standing outside a green-painted wooden shack, the word Mambo's painted on the side in bright, graffiti-style letters. I glance at my watch and as it's just after nine o'clock, I glance around the outside space for Chloe and Amy.

'Orla, over here.' Amy waves.

The girls are sat at one of the benches in the seating area decked out in fake grass, wooden benches and lights threaded through the surrounding white fence. They are sat at a long table with several other people, sipping delicious-looking cocktails with fruit and straws poking out. They squeeze along the bench to make room for me. Both of the girls are wearing tiny mini dresses – Chloe in black and Amy's white – and have perfect make-up and eyebrows. As I sit down, the other people smile at me in greeting as the girls introduce me.

'You've just missed it,' says Chloe, before taking a sip of her pina colada. 'A couple were having a right old go at each other, weren't they, Ames?'

'Yeah.' Amy picks up the story. 'This attractive girl walks up to the guy, who was with his girlfriend, and throws her arms around him. She was like "I can't believe you're here again this year. Why did you stop messaging me when you got home?"'

'So then, the girl he was with completely lost it. Apparently, they'd been together for three years when he'd come here last year on a stag do.'

'Yeah, she told him she was thinking of dumping him anyway, because he was dragging his feet over buying a place together,' continues Chloe. 'Shouting their business all over the bar they were, it was better than an episode of *EastEnders*. I half expected the bar owner to come out and say, "Get out of my pub."' Chloe laughs.

'And then,' says Amy. 'She tipped the last of her cocktail all over his nice white shirt. The air was blue.'

'So was his shirt, it was a Blue Lagoon,' Chloe adds, laughing once more, along with the people sat nearby.

Listening to the story of the warring couple makes me grateful that I'm happily single. Although it works for many people, I've never been tempted to try online dating. I'm not keen on relationships at work, even though they do say that seventy per cent of people meet in the workplace – I do wonder what you would talk about in the evenings. How was your day? Not something you would need to ask. I'd never been in one job long enough to meet anyone either – there was Pascha from the circus, of course, but that didn't work. I'm also not much of a pub goer, preferring cosy cafés and picnics, so I guess I'm limiting myself there a little too. And, especially since my illness, I've been concentrating on just looking after myself, and don't feel I need the complication of getting involved with someone new.

I order a glass of white wine from a waitress bringing drinks out to the rest of the table, resolutely determined not to mix drinks despite the tasty-looking cocktails. Not after the last time, when I was out partying with an ex, mixed my drinks, got slaughtered and accidentally climbed into bed with his younger brother on the way back from the bathroom in the middle of the night.

I'm having such a fun evening, I can't remember the last time I let my hair down and had such a good night. I'm determined to enjoy myself, but at the same time I don't want to overdo things. I'm just sitting down after a dance, having a sip of my drink, when a handsome guy everyone seems to know pushes his way through the crowds towards the bar. I realise when he gets closer that it's Captain Jack.

'Ahoy there,' I say before adding, 'Sorry, I bet you've never heard that one before.'

Flashing me his dazzling smile, he says, 'Hi, how are you doing?' His tan looks even deeper tonight, his blonde streaks blonder.

'I met you at the beach bar,' I remind him, not sure he recognises me.

'I know who you arrr,' he says in his pirate voice. 'Okay that's enough of that, I'm off duty. It's Orla, isn't it? Can I get you a drink?'

'It is. And a Coke would be nice, thanks.'

I'm already feeling a little merry and feel another drink would only tip me over the edge.

I follow Jack inside to the bar, festooned with fake palm trees, with a green light flashing across a wooden dance floor. A DJ is playing his set from the corner of the room and Chloe and Amy are still going for it on the dance floor.

My Coke is served with lots of ice and a slice of lemon, and Jack orders a pint of cold beer before we head outside again. Amy catches my eye as we walk past, and gives me a thumbs up sign, before continuing to dance wildly with a tall bloke with dreadlocks.

'So, how has your evening been?' I ask, sipping the drink

and enjoying a welcome breeze coming from the sea across the road.

'Brilliant, actually. The boat was full, and we had a really good crowd,' he tells me.

'No drunks walking the plank then?'

'No, thank goodness.' He smiles that megawatt smile again. 'How about you? Are you having a good time?'

'Lovely thanks. Unexpected too. I kind of thought I'd have a meal, then head back to the hotel and have a read. I know that might sound really boring, but I've been taking things easy,' I say, although not revealing any more. 'Anyway, drinks were mentioned, and I thought, what the heck. I'm on holiday.'

'Well, I'm glad you came out.' He lifts his beer and clinks it against my glass. 'This is my bar of choice when I've finished work. I really like the vibe here.'

We chat easily for a while and after he's had a second drink, he says he's heading off.

'Are you going my way? I could walk you back to your hotel if you like,' he offers.

'Where are you staying?' I ask.

'On the boat,' he tells me. 'I live there.'

'You live there?' I say in surprise.

'Yep. I own the boat so it makes sense. Below deck is really cosy. I suppose it's like living on a houseboat but with more visitors.' He laughs. 'Although I only do that during high season. In the quieter months, I moor the boat up and rent an apartment across town with a friend who works the summer season in a restaurant, so we split the rent.'

'Sounds like the perfect life.'

Glancing across the road, the foaming sea rolling onto the sand and lights from distant islands glowing and a beautiful silver moon in the sky, I wonder what it would be like to actually live in a place like this.

'I don't suppose anyone's life is perfect.' He shrugs. 'Money can be a little tight in the winter months but it suits me. For now, at least.'

Finishing my drink, I decide to take Jack up on his offer of walking me to my hotel, so head inside to say goodnight to the girls.

EIGHT

Walking home together, we pass the restaurants in full swing, the sound of laughter coming from them as well as the tantalising smells wafting into the evening air. Smiling waiters say goodnight at the entrance to some customers. Couples are spilling out of bars, some slightly the worse for wear. We pass a music bar, its sign lit up in pink lights, with dance music pumping out.

I don't suppose I've ever really been a nightclub sort of person. I always preferred bars with live music and going to music festivals, especially local ones with up-and-coming artists. There's something about music that I can really lose myself in.

During my recovery, I spent hours listening to uplifting music and jazz while I was recuperating. Music and television became my salvation. As well as drawing, which became a little bit of a hobby after my operation. I drew mainly birds with colourful plumage, hopping into the garden. I was surprised by the amount of bird visitors to the garden, although I suppose it's something you only notice when you slow down and observe what is actually going on in the world around you. When you stop to smell the roses, the coffee, or whatever it is you prefer. I would never have thought of observing birds and sketching them, but during my illness I felt in tune with nature somehow, feeling the need to capture something of the world around me. Funnily enough, I haven't drawn since recovering, although I do think about it occasionally and really ought to buy some decent pencils and paper. After my operation, I noticed everything around me with heightened senses, feeling an appreciation of the world that I hadn't really felt before. Dad framed some of my sketches of blue tits and robins and hung them in the hallway in dark frames, which makes me feel kind of proud that he thought them good enough to put on display.

'Well, this is me,' I tell Jack, stopping outside the hotel, set back a little from the harbour front. Despite being not far from the noise of lines of bars, restaurants and shops, it's so quiet that the distinctive sound of crickets in a nearby hedge can be heard.

'See you then. And you know where I am if you fancy a boat trip,' Jack says.

'I do. Thanks for walking me home, Jack. See you around then.'

'No problem. See you.' He smiles, before heading off to his boat.

I head through the front door to reception and find Sophia emerging from the kitchen carrying a tray of something.

'*Kalispera*, Orla. Have you had a nice evening?' She's dressed in a cerise-coloured lounge suit, her hair pinned up. She's wearing no make-up, yet still looks effortlessly glamorous.

'Lovely, thanks.'

'We're just having a nightcap outside if you would care to join us. It's such a beautiful evening.'

'Um sure, okay, thanks.' I follow her to the garden outside, where the American guests are sat at a table, along with Theo. There is a small fire pit glowing in the dark, the silvery moon set in an inky sky above.

Sophia orders Theo to fetch another brandy from the bar

for me. Despite my protestations that a soft drink would suffice, he jumps up to fetch one.

'This evening I am being shown how to make s'mores,' says Sophia. 'I can't say it's something I've ever tried before. Or even heard of.'

'Then you don't know what you're missing out on,' says Brady, taking a marshmallow from the bag on the tray, and threading it onto a bamboo skewer.

'These biscuits look mighty fine too.' He takes what look like giant digestive biscuits with a chocolate covering from a bag.

We each take a marshmallow and toast it over the fire pit, as instructed, before pressing it between the crunchy biscuits.

'Oh my goodness.' Sophia is in raptures over the simple dessert, and I silently devour mine, reminded of toasting marshmallows at bonfire night as a child.

'Aren't you indulging?' I ask Theo, who has re-joined us with my brandy.

'It's not worth it. A few of those would take an extra two-mile run along the beach to work off,' he says, resisting the tasty treat.

His fitness regime is obviously paying off, I can't help noticing. His black T-shirt shows off his toned flat stomach and muscular arms.

'This is true,' says his mother. 'Although you should not deny yourself anything. Everything in moderation is the key,' she says, before adding, 'Oh what the hell,' and spearing another marshmallow with a wooden skewer and toasting it.

We discuss our days, and Brady and Iris tell us that they have been to a hammam and spa in Tigaki.

'What a place,' says Iris. 'We had the most luxurious massage, didn't we, Brady?' Her husband nods as he devours his third s'more.

'The place is just wonderful,' she continues. 'As well as the massage rooms and saunas, there's a vitamin bar and a hair-dressing studio. I had my nails done too.' She displays her perfect nails. 'The shade is sunset gold. I kind of think it matches my hair.' She touches her hair that she tells us she had washed and blow-dried, whilst Brady enjoyed a second massage. 'For his back problem.'

Chloe and Amy are still out, and there's been no sign of Georgios the writer. I sip at a brandy, feeling the burn, and relax as we discuss our plans for the rest of the holiday.

Iris and Brady are heading out on a jeep safari tomorrow after their relaxing day today, and I think I might take the car out and do a little exploring myself. I can't help noticing Theo looks a little bored and I wonder why he isn't out on the town himself. But then, maybe it's because he has an early start, helping his mother with the breakfasts in the morning. He does have a job in a hotel after all, so maybe leaves his partying until the weekend. He stretches his arms over his head and stands.

'I will bid you *kalinychta*,' he says before heading off.

Everyone is in good spirits enjoying the s'mores party and nightcap, although it is getting rather warm with the heat of the fire pit, especially on a night as warm as this. We all laugh along to something Brady has just said, when the sound of a patio door from above being forcefully slammed can be heard. It's the room next door to mine.

'And that,' says Sophia, standing up, 'is where the evening ends. I cannot have guests disapproving. It is getting a little late, I suppose.' She nods towards the room next to mine.

Glancing at my watch, I'm surprised to find that it's just after midnight. I offer to help Sophia tidy away as the others say goodnight and filter off to their bedroom.

'I take it you don't need much sleep then,' I comment as we carry some glasses and plates to the dishwasher, where she loads them.

'Five hours is more than enough,' she replies. 'And as breakfast isn't served until eight, I have plenty of time for my beauty sleep.'

'I'm no good with anything short of seven hours. Preferably eight. Goodnight, then. See you in the morning.'

'*Kalinychta*, Orla, and thank you.'

Letting myself into my room, I think about Georgios slamming his patio door shut. I hope this place works its magic, and he allows himself to relax a little. How could this beautiful island not bring inspiration to a writer, I wonder? Then again, I expect it depends on the type of book he is writing. I also imagine Chloe and Amy somewhere in a nightclub, having the time of their life and find myself smiling. Life is for living, whichever way you choose that to be. I can hardly wait until tomorrow to see what adventure it brings!

NINE

I wake early the next morning, so decide to head across to the beach for the morning yoga session. I quickly dress in a pair of shorts and a cropped top, and carrying a towel – in the absence of a yoga mat – I quietly let myself out of the hotel and head across the road to the beach.

It's so peaceful at this hour, the sun just rising and the streets empty in complete contrast to the bustling scene last night. Litter pickers make their way along the beach road, and trucks are negotiating backstreets as they make early morning deliveries to bars and restaurants. I head down the stone steps to the beach and join around a dozen other people of varying ages who have arrived for the yoga session. It seems I've arrived at just the right time, as the class is about to begin.

'Hi there, Orla, and welcome to the class.'

Theo is dressed in grey lounge pants and a white vest as he walks towards me and greets me. Rose, who I met at the beach bar, waves and I take a place next to her and lay my towel down.

'You might be better with this,' says Theo, unzipping a long black holdall and retrieving a purple yoga mat that he hands to me.

'Thanks! You never mentioned at the hotel that you were a yoga teacher?'

'You never asked.' He shrugs, a smile on his face.

There's a calmness and beauty watching the sun fully rise here on the gorgeous beach, and Theo is an excellent teacher, effortlessly putting us through gentle stretches followed by more strenuous poses.

'And from downward dog, into upward dog,' he calls out as we follow his instruction.

During the relaxation and cooling down part of the class, the sound of the waves gently lapping the sand relaxes and simultaneously energises every muscle in my body and I struggle to keep my eyes open.

It's not long before the class is over and Theo joins hands and wishes us, 'Namaste.'

'That was fantastic, Theo. Thank you,' I say, feeling wonderful and ready for the day ahead.

'I'm glad you enjoyed it. Are you walking back for breakfast at the hotel?' he asks, picking up his bag.

'In a little while. I fancy a walk along the beach first.'

'See you back there then,' he says, walking off across the sand.

Walking along, feeling the soft sand between my toes, I feel so lucky to be alive. I find myself thinking of all the jobs I had as a young woman, never really settling anywhere. Potters was the first job I ever felt the desire to stay at, but, thinking about it, that is mostly down to the warmness of my workmates. After my tumour was diagnosed, even that started to feel a little claustrophobic and I wish I knew why I felt this way. I glance out across the vast Aegean Sea and feel so small, wondering what my purpose is in the universe. They say we all have a purpose. I'm sure I will find mine soon enough, grateful to be given the chance to discover it.

Rose, who has been chatting to another woman, calls my name and catches up with me.

'Hey, Rose. How are things going?' I ask.

'Pretty good, actually. I have a telephone appointment with my doctor later this afternoon to discuss my HRT,' she tells me candidly. 'Theo is a marvellous instructor, but he's so hot it's a distraction.' She laughs. 'Oh, listen to me, you must think I'm a right old lush.' She laughs again.

'Not at all.' In truth, I could do with a little of her joie de vivre as I haven't felt sexually attracted to a bloke in a while. Although I guess I haven't been feeling too well of late.

A beach bar is just opening up for breakfast, so I join Rose for a glass of fresh orange juice, before leaving her with her breakfast of fruits and yoghurt and head back to the hotel to have some breakfast there.

'See you at yoga again. Maybe in a couple of days though. I have a feeling I'm going to have aching muscles in the morning,' I joke with her as I leave.

After a quick shower, I walk outside into the blazing sunshine. Breakfast is laid out on the long table near the pool, covered with a large gazebo. It's so full, set with meats and cheeses as well as Greek yoghurt, honey, bread rolls and figs. Pots full of fresh apple and orange juice and tea and coffee are laid out too. Iris and Brady are the only two people sat at the table, with no sign of Chloe, Amy, or the mysterious author.

'Good morning.' I take a seat opposite Iris, after filling a glass with some apple juice.

'Kalimera,' says Sophia, brandishing a coffee pot. I politely decline, sticking to juice.

We're enjoying breakfast, discussing our plans for the day, when Amy and Chloe finally emerge looking the worse for wear. There's still no sign of Georgios though. Maybe he has been working through the night and is enjoying a lie-in.

'Morning.' Chloe fills a tumbler of orange juice and glugs it down as Amy goes for the apple juice.

'Late night, girls?' I ask as Chloe stifles a yawn.

'Too late. Never again.' Amy lets out a deep sigh as she clutches her head.

'Yeah right,' Chloe replies, laughing. 'Until the next time.'

They nibble at some bread half-heartedly, barely saying a word as Brady and Iris finish their breakfast, and set off to enjoy their day.

'Is my neighbour not joining us then?' I ask Sophia as she piles some plates onto a tray.

'No. He has taken breakfast in his room,' she informs me. 'It seems he really is a very private person.'

After breakfast, I head upstairs and take my book outside onto my balcony for a while, until I decide what I am going to do for the rest of the day. My balcony gives a view of the sea in the distance and some of the tall palm trees on the harbour front. I could sit here for hours reading and enjoying the view if I weren't so keen to explore everything Kos Town has to offer. Sat on the next balcony is Georgios, who's sipping a coffee and staring at his laptop. He's wearing a white linen shirt, the sleeves rolled up and his sunglasses pushed to the top of his black, slightly curly hair.

'Good morning,' I say brightly.

'Oh, good morning.' He lifts his head and gives a smile, which even though it's strained, transforms his whole face.

'How's the writing going?' I tentatively ask.

'It isn't.' He lets out a deep sigh. 'I came here thinking it might inspire me. My grandparents are always telling me, "Come to Greece, how can you not be inspired here."' He turns to look at me with his striking dark-brown eyes. 'I managed the first few chapters back home, but then... Nothing.'

'Your grandparents live here?'

'Yes, they own the restaurant we both dined at last night,' he informs me.

'That really is a fantastic restaurant. Was that your sister who worked there?' I ask.

'That's right, yes. Her name is Helena. Now, if you'll excuse me, I really must get on.' His tone is a little clipped, so I return to my book as he picks up his laptop and heads inside his room.

'Sure, bye then.'

Maybe next time, I'll tell him about Theo's yoga classes on the beach. It might just loosen him up a bit. He could certainly do with it.

I'm enjoying my own book, an historical fiction piece set in a Scottish castle, when my phone rings. It's Dad.

'Hi, Dad! How are you?' It feels so good to hear his voice.

'Good thanks, love. More importantly, how are you?'

'Oh, I'm fine, thanks. The hotel is lovely and so are the guests here. I do feel lucky that they are such a nice bunch of people.'

I do seem to be blessed with meeting nice people these days.

'Glad to hear it, although you always make friends wherever you go, so I wasn't worried about that.'

Apart from with the surly guy next door that is, which I don't mention. Dad tells me he is off to Llandudno with some of his golf buddies at the weekend.

'A few games of golf and the hotel we've booked into is on the seafront. They have an entertainment programme in the evening too.' He sounds pretty excited. 'I think they've got Chubby Checker one night, he was big in the sixties.'

'Hence his name?'

'No, I mean a big hit. He was tall and slim, actually, funny that.' He chuckles.

'It all sounds like a lot of fun, Dad. I hope you have a lovely time.'

'I'm sure I will, thanks, love. You look after yourself.'

I'm so happy Dad has been able to get on with his life since Mum passed, as I'm sure it's what she would have wanted. In fact, I'm certain of it. When she was ill, she told him she didn't want him to be alone in his older years. That was typical of Mum, always thinking of others before herself. I can't help wondering what she would have made of the situation I uncovered in Dad's letter before heading out here. Perhaps her benevolence might not have stretched that far, but I guess we will never know.

Finishing the call, I decide to drive into Kefalos and have a walk along the beach. It has one long sandy beach with clear shallow waters, just perfect for swimming. I pack my beachwear into a straw bag that matches my hat, looking forward to a swim in the warm sea. After that, I might head to the Casa Romana, a perfectly preserved Roman house and museum that attracts a lot of visitors. I've visited before, but even so I still enjoy stepping onto the mosaic floors, exploring the rooms and Roman sculptures, enjoying the feeling of stepping back in time. I could spend a whole afternoon browsing the ancient artefacts on display.

Annoyingly, I've packed an out-of-date sun cream, so I nip out to a local supermarket. As I'm walking, I spot Amy and Chloe sitting at an outside café table wearing sunglasses and tucking into a full English breakfast.

'Don't worry, I won't tell Sophia you think her breakfasts are awful,' I say, passing their table.

'Orla, hi! I was craving a full English, to be honest. They've even got the brown HP Sauce,' Chloe says, pointing to a bottle on the table, before cutting into a pork sausage.

'Your secret is safe with me.' I wink. 'Although, you know, I'm pretty sure she might have made you a cooked breakfast if you'd asked.'

'I dunno. Her breakfasts look far too healthy. Don't get me wrong, any other day, that's fine. But this morning, well, I really needed this,' says Amy. 'It's the best hangover cure ever. It's those cocktails that did it.' She shakes her head. 'Never again.'

'What are you up to today then?' asks Chloe, so I tell her about Kefalos.

'We're off on the pirate boat trip later, it might be a laugh.'

'Only because you think the pirate guy is fit,' Amy says, giggling.

'You mean Jack?' I say.

'You know him?' asks Chloe in surprise.

'I do. I was chatting to him at Mambo's last night.'

'Oh my gosh, was that him? I didn't recognise him; it was a little dark inside. Are you two an item then?'

'What? No, I only got chatting to him yesterday at a beach bar. He walked me home, but it's not like that,' I tell her. 'I'm happily single, and I assume he is too.'

'Right, well we're definitely going on that boat trip then,' she decides, looking suddenly revitalised. 'Maybe you could join us later, if you fancy it too? We're going to chill around the pool at the hotel first to work on our tan for a couple of hours.'

'I'm not sure,' I say doubtfully. 'I don't really have good sea legs, although maybe I will if I'm around. What time are you talking?'

'There's a four-thirty sailing, we'll probably go for that,' says Chloe.

'Well, if I don't join you, have a great time,' I tell them as I head off.

I get my sun cream and soon I'm driving along the coast road towards Kefalos, passing the usual shops and restaurants en route. People are sat on balconies above shops watching the world go by and mopeds are weaving in and out of the busy traffic. It's mid-July so the middle of high season, and Kos is bustling with tourists. Rubbing shoulders with the shops are some beautiful apartments with sand-coloured walls and black-metal fences on balconies. Occasionally, I glimpse a side street of white-painted houses with blue shutters and mopeds parked outside.

Driving on, I pass a shop with a lime-green front, making it stand out from the shops all around it and a rush of memories come flooding back. It's like an Aladdin's cave inside, and sells just about anything you can think of, in long narrow aisles packed with goods. It's the kind of place where you go in looking for one particular item and come out with a bag full of things you probably don't need. I remember shopping there with Mum, while Dad had a game of mini golf with a bloke he'd met at the hotel. She bought me a sparkly pink phone cover for my first-ever mobile phone. My parents weren't keen on me having a phone at all from what I remember, but as all my friends had one, they finally relented and I got one for Christmas, which wasn't long before my thirteenth birthday.

I stop at traffic lights, and a group of teenagers cross en masse, earbuds plugged in, giggling and jostling each other. I sit watching them as I wait for the lights to change, thinking how quickly time passes. It doesn't seem like five minutes since I was dancing at my first festival at the age of sixteen at a local farmer's field and had my first kiss with a boy I'd liked at school. I take the time to retrieve a compact from my bag and reapply a slick of pink cotton-candy lipstick before the teenagers finally reach the other side of the zebra crossing.

Arriving in Kefalos, I park up and sigh with pleasure when I take in the soft, creamy-coloured sand on a beach that seems to go on forever. I glance at the little island across the water, with a small church on it, and think I might swim across there next time I come here. But today I'll settle for a little paddle in the water to cool off.

After paying a guy for a sunbed, I take a selfie of myself with the sea in the background and send it to Polly. Within seconds she's replied with a text.

That's not fair! X

Accompanied by a photo of herself sitting near a window in the office, where it appears to be pouring down. A new message pops up.

I'll call you in a bit on my lunch break. X

I buy a cooling fresh orange juice from a beach shack before settling down on my sunbed to continue with a little reading. There's a young couple lying on the sunbeds just over from mine, and as the bloke massages sun oil into his partner, the scent of coconut permeates the air. There are so many loved-up couples everywhere that I wonder if I've stumbled upon a couples only beach.

I snuggle down onto my bed and think about the last boyfriend I had, which was a few years ago. Todd was a biker, and we had a ball zipping along country roads in the Lake District and going to bike meets with some of his friends. We had such fun during the long, hazy days of summer, picnicking on beaches and camping beneath the stars. I remember riding along roads high in the fells, the wind blowing through my hair without a care in the world. I was having the time of my life. That was before Todd began talking of settling down, maybe buying an apartment near the coast. As much as I loved him, I just couldn't. I suddenly felt caged in, the thought of committing to a mortgage terrifying. We argued and he said that 'normal' people put down roots and why was it such a big issue to me? I couldn't answer him. After two years, we parted ways and he told me I had issues with commitment and that maybe I ought to go and talk to someone about it.

I thought about his comments long after we split, and although I missed him, I knew I'd done the right thing. I'd flitted from jobs and boyfriends most of my life. Maybe Todd was right about my commitment issues. Or perhaps I was just having a good time; I was only young after all. Maybe I hadn't yet met the love of my life so I wasn't prepared to settle for anything less. Surely, we shouldn't be expected to? I'd seen too many friends marry young, becoming trapped in unhappy marriages before splitting up and leaving their children miserable and confused. And considering what I found, maybe my own parents' marriage wasn't as happy as I had always believed it to be...

I'm mulling these things over when my phone rings and Polly's face flashes up onto the screen for a video call.

'Polly, hi! I see you're in the office again?' I say, noting her surroundings.

'Yep. I've taken the job in the office full time,' she says with a beaming smile.

'Brilliant! Good for you. How's it going?' I ask, really pleased for her.

'It's great. I really like working in the office. I've been reorganising the filing system, and re-labelling all of the manual files. You know what a neat freak I am,' she admits.

I definitely do. Polly even has her books lined up in her bookcase at home with the names of the authors displayed alphabetically. She's also organised them by genre and colour.

'I was going to message you tomorrow, I wanted to give you a chance to settle in. So, what's it like there then?' she asks.

'Oh, you know, I can't complain.'

I pan my phone around to show her the wonderful beach, just as two muscular lifeguards in red shorts and wearing shades stroll into view.

'Wow, I'm not jealous at all.' She laughs.

'Don't you have Tim? How are things going there?' I ask and I see her blush a little, easily noticeable against her red hair.

'Things are going really well, actually,' she says, sounding a tiny bit excited. 'I'm a bit nervous about having a relationship with the boss though. I hope things don't get awkward if it doesn't work out between us.'

'I wouldn't worry about that. Even if things didn't work out, which I can't see why they wouldn't, Tim's a nice guy. Try not to worry, just take one day at a time,' I advise.

'You're right. I wish I was more laid-back like you.' She sighs. 'I guess I've always been a bit of a worrier.'

'I wasn't always this way. Having a brain tumour kind of makes you revaluate things in life. And if it taught me anything, it's that you should live life one day at a time. Worrying is bad for your health.'

'Well, I can't argue with that.' She smiles, lighting up her pretty face.

Polly fills me in on the office news, although there isn't really much to report. Things are ticking over nicely and the larger shoe range is still doing well. She tells me kindly that people are missing me and I promise to call in and say hi to everyone as soon as I get home.

A couple of hours later, after a delicious lunch of grilled fish and Greek salad, I take a short drive to the Roman villa. Entering its cool interior I wander the rooms imagining the people from a bygone era walking across these very mosaic floors. When I've finished exploring the villa, rich with historical artefacts and interesting sculptures, I step outside into a pretty courtyard and hear the unmistakeable voices of Brady and Iris.

'Don't you just love these places?' says Iris with a deep sigh, staring up at the fine stone-coloured building that has long windows, and overlooks a pretty courtyard, filled with terracotta urns bursting with colourful flowers.

'Hi, guys, what are you doing here?'

'Oh, hey there, Orla.' Brady smiles when he notices me. 'It's a stop off on the jeep tour,' he says, mopping his brow with a handkerchief. 'It's one helluva hot day though, I'm kinda looking forward to the breeze as we drive along in the open-topped jeep.' He chuckles.

'Isn't it wonderful,' says Iris, who's looking pretty in a pink linen shift. 'This is why we love coming to Greece. We just don't have this kind of history in America. We're thinking about Jordan next year, I would just love to see that Lost City of Petra,' she says, and Brady nods in agreement.

A young Greek man, wearing a navy shirt with Zeus Tours emblazoned across it in white writing, rounds up the tourists as they prepare to head off for their next stop.

'Next stop is a late lunch at a taverna in a forest,' says Brady, smiling broadly. 'Should be nice and cool, near the lake.'

'See you later, enjoy the rest of your tour,' I say as they head to a row of four parked white jeeps that quickly drive off in convoy.

Glancing at my watch, I notice it's just after three thirty, so I decide to drive back to the harbour in Kos Town. Maybe I will join Amy and Chloe in that boat trip out on Captain Jack's boat after all. I think it might be quite entertaining to watch him in action, brandishing his sword for the entertainment of the tourists.

TEN

The roads seem a little emptier on the return journey, so I relax and enjoy the drive, appreciating the view of the sparkling sea that seems to stretch on forever. I notice a group of women wearing pink T-shirts with the words 'Hens on tour' printed across the back and the bride-to-be wearing a tiara. I can't help thinking how young they all look and hope the bride gets her happy ever after. I suppose it can happen for some couples. My mum and dad had the most wonderful marriage, with hardly ever a cross word between them as I recall, but maybe they kept their cross words for when I was out of earshot. There were a few things they didn't really go into with me. When I was young, Dad did go away for a while and I really missed him. I was around six years old, and his absence was never really explained at the time, although I remember Mum vaguely telling me he had a job somewhere far away. When he finally returned, we took our very first holiday to Kos.

But, even in their later years, I would hear them in the kitchen giggling at something silly together. Maybe they set the benchmarks for my relationship expectations, which is maybe why I wouldn't settle for anything. Until quite recently, I believed my parents had the perfect marriage, although I guess nothing is perfect, and any flaws in a marriage would surely be easy to shield from a young child. I never want to settle down with someone if I don't believe it will last.

Approaching Kos Town, the view of the boats in the harbour come into view and I see Jack's wooden pirate boat at the quayside, towering above the other tourist boats, its ladder and crow's nest visible along with the skull and crossbones flag waving gently in the sea breeze.

I park the car back at the hotel, before taking the five-minute walk back to the boat. As I approach the harbour front, I spot Amy and Chloe sat at a bar nearby with a dark-haired bloke wearing a T-shirt advertising Jack's boat trips.

'Orla!' Amy waves me over when she notices me.

'This is Mike, he works on the pirate boat,' says Chloe, introducing the bloke sat beside her.

'The other half of the sword-fighting duo.' He laughs, taking a sip of coffee.

'Hi, Mike, pleased to meet you. What's your alter ego then?' I ask as I take a seat, before ordering a cold beer.

'Blackbeard. Seeing as I already have one.' He laughs again, stroking his rather impressive beard. 'Although it's not usually this long,' he adds. He's handsome and his charming manner seems to have captivated Amy, who is hanging on to his every word.

'Right, that's me.' He stands to leave. 'I need to head over to the boat and get changed. We sail shortly, see you there, ladies. I hope you will be joining us, Orla.'

'See you, Mike.' Amy crosses her slender, tanned legs, which Mike's eyes flick over, I can't help noticing.

The three of us are chatting away, when Rose walks past and joins us, going for a coffee instead of beer. After introductions are made, Chloe persuades her to join us on the cruise, despite her initial apprehension and some protest that it wasn't really her thing. I'm still not quite sure it's mine.

We're all chatting away like old friends, when out of the corner of my eye, I see a bloke on his own strolling along the harbour, stopping to occasionally admire a boat, and I realise it's Georgios.

'Excuse me for one moment.' I head away from the group, and catch up with him as he walks on.

'Hi, Georgios.' I smile and he returns it, looking in a slightly better mood today.

'Hi, Orla. How are you?'

'I'm good, thanks. You? How's the book coming along?' I ask brightly.

'Not much better.' He shrugs. 'Although I have managed to get a few pages written, which is something. I'm hoping being out and about will give me some inspiration. It definitely can't do any harm.'

He looks gorgeous in a white polo shirt, dark shorts and navy loafers. I notice he's wearing a leather bracelet at his wrist in an olive-green colour. His slightly curly hair rests on his shoulders.

'I thought about what you said about going outside and getting away from my laptop for a while. Although my heart hasn't been in my writing just lately, if I'm honest,' he tells me, not going into the reason why. 'One thing is for sure though. Sitting staring at my computer wasn't inspiring me to get a single word down.'

'Sometimes you just need to get away and clear your head. It's what I do when I'm faced with a problem. And you never know, you might just come across something you can write about.' I try for a positive voice.

'You are right.' Georgios smiles. 'Sometimes you just need to clear your head. I'll definitely get the book finished though. I always do.'

'I'm sure your editor will be pleased to hear that,' I add.

He turns to face me, those gorgeous dark-brown eyes boring into me.

'I told you about my editor?' He has a puzzled look on his face.

'Um, no. I kind of overheard you in the restaurant,' I confess, looking a little sheepish.

'So, you were eavesdropping?' he asks, but he's smiling.

'Not eavesdropping exactly. I was at a nearby table remember, and your editor wasn't exactly talking quietly. And the restaurant was a little quiet because it was quite early in the evening.' I think I am over-explaining things.

'Then you'll know that my editor is on my case.' He sighs. 'I thought locking myself away would help me to focus but, of course, you can't force these things.'

'Worrying about it will only make it worse,' I say cheerfully, before realising it maybe wasn't the right thing to say. 'Anyway,' I add quickly. 'As you're out and about, why don't you come and say hello to my new friends?'

'Sure, okay,' he says, much to my surprise as he walks with me back to join my friends.

'Is Georgios a Greek name?' I find myself asking as we walk along.

'Yes, it is. My father was keen on a traditional Greek name but I think my mother wanted more of an English-sounding name like George, so they compromised and settled on Georgios.'

When we arrive at the table outside the bar, everyone is introduced and Rose takes her fan from her bag and wafts it in front of her face. When Georgios heads to the bar, Amy pounces.

'Oh my gosh, is that the mysterious guy from the hotel in the room next to yours?' she asks, her eyes wide.

'The very same.'

'What a shame he doesn't come down to the pool and socialise. He is seriously hot,' she says.

'He's not the only one,' adds Rose, flapping her fan violently in front of her face and making us laugh.

Georgios returns from the bar with a frappé and Amy tells him we're boarding the pirate ship in ten minutes for a trip around the bay. 'They're stopping at a little island for a BBQ too. You should come along,' she says.

'Sounds lovely. I'm not sure it's my thing though. It will probably be full of overexcited children.' He takes a sip of his frappé.

'I was thinking the same thing,' says Rose. 'But you know what? Holidays are all about having new experiences, aren't they?' she says, before lowering her sunglasses and staring at him, with a seductive smile.

'I guess so,' says Georgios, visibly shifting uneasily in his seat, which makes me inwardly laugh, especially when I stare at Chloe and Amy, who are sat there open-mouthed.

'Right, come on then.' Amy bangs her glass down on the table decisively. 'We'd better get going, or us landlubbers will be left behind.'

We take the short walk to the pirate ship and take our seats on long padded benches aboard the surprisingly spacious vessel, to the strains of a sea shanty being played in the background, through speakers. The rest of the passengers are already seated and say hi as we join them.

As I take a seat, I realise that even though the boat is still moored up, it is gently rocking back and forth. Maybe I should have taken a seasickness pill before setting off.

Once we are all sat comfortably, Jack bounces onto the scrubbed deck in full pirate gear, looking fantastic, quickly followed by Mike, who looks amazing too. Captain Jack and Blackbeard introduce themselves to the crowd, the excited children jumping up and down with joy as they go through their act. A young girl is thrilled when they suggest her older brother walk the plank if she can tell them why she thinks he deserves it, while the boy shakes his head, denying any wrongdoing and laughing.

Setting sail across the water, we soon leave the harbour behind and the other crew members, in stripy red-and-white T-shirts and black trousers, serve us with drinks. The children are invited to take it in turns to steer the ship's wheel, guided by Jack Sparrow, along with one or two of the dads who are keen to have a go too. There are songs and jollity, and the much-antici-pated sword fight is the highlight of the outward journey. Jack and Mike really are nimble on their feet, swashbuckling their way around the wooden floor of the boat, delighting children and adults alike. As they take a bow at the end of the perfor-mance, they receive rousing applause and a standing ovation.

Thankfully my stomach has settled a little, and when the small beach is in sight, I realise I am a little hungry.

'Well, that was amazing,' I say to Jack as he approaches our group. 'I almost didn't recognise you with your clothes on,' I tell him, which draws an audible gasp from Rose.

'That's what all the girls say,' he replies, laughing, and Georgios, who is stood next to me, looks surprised.

'I meant minus his pirate gear,' I explain, blushing as I realise that sounds even worse.

'Too much information.' Georgios lifts his hands and smiles, his gorgeous grin once again lighting up his whole face.

Flushed with embarrassment, I find myself telling Georgios how I met Jack at the beach bar when I first arrived here and have seen him around a few times since I've been here.

As the children continue to take it in turns at the ship's wheel under the watchful eye of Captain Jack, I can see Georgios smiling at them, and can't help wondering if he has any children of his own. The kids examine a fake cannon on deck and ask Jack lots of questions, which he answers in character.

He clearly knows a lot, as he regales them with stories of pirates pillaging passing ships.

A short while later, the boat drops its anchor in the glorious blue-green water, close to a sandy cove, that has mountains rising in the background and Jack makes an announcement saying he will drop the ladder for anyone who wants to swim to the nearby beach. He informs us all that we will spend around an hour and a half to enjoy a swim and a BBQ before we return to the harbour at Kos.

Amy and Chloe remove their kaftans, revealing their toned tan bodies in tiny bikinis and climb down a rope ladder into the inviting water. They are followed by several other people who had clearly come prepared for the journey, unlike me and several others. Rose, Georgios and I, along with a middle-aged couple, stay on board as Jack and Mike lean on the side of the boat, chatting to Amy and Chloe, who are splashing about in the water. Chloe asks Jack if he is sure there are no sharks in these waters and he reassures her there are none.

'It's the ones on land you have to careful of,' shouts a bloke in the water, and everyone laughs.

'What do you do for a living?' Rose asks Georgios as we chat on board, sipping a cooling drink.

'I'm a writer,' he reveals. 'Although I'm not sure I can even call myself that at the moment.'

'A writer, really? How interesting,' says Rose. 'Are you currently writing something?'

'Attempting to, yes.' He sighs.

'Well, I wouldn't worry. All authors get a bit of writer's block, don't they?' she says. 'But surely there's inspiration here?'

She points to the lush green islands in the background of the sparkling sea, and the creamy stretch of sandy beach behind us.

'You would think so,' says Georgios, sounding a little strained once more. 'It's what everybody seems to tell me.'

'You're so lucky. I'd love to be sat on a balcony somewhere, earning my living by writing,' says Rose, clearly not picking up on his mood. 'It sounds like a dream job.' She sighs.

'Actually, if you'll excuse me for a moment.' Georgios stands up. 'Oh and I'd rather you kept the fact that I'm an author quiet, if you don't mind.' He walks over to Jack and Mike, where he strikes up a conversation with them.

'Oh dear, was it something I said?' Rose sips her orange juice through a black-and-white striped straw.

'I don't think so. I just get the impression he doesn't want to speak about his work too much. He's a bit stressed, I think. He has a deadline to meet.'

'These creative types can be so temperamental. What genre does he write?' she asks, clearly intrigued.

'Do you know, I haven't asked him. He hasn't exactly been forthcoming about it, so I thought I'd leave him to relax a bit.'

'Understandable. Well, I'm sure he will soon be relaxed and raring to write,' she says, before removing her sunglasses and holding her face up to the sun. 'I still think it's a dream job though. Maybe he ought to count his lucky stars.'

ELEVEN

When we head down the gangplank to the beach, some of the swimmers are sitting on large flat rocks drying off under the hot sun; others are still splashing about in the crystal-clear water. A BBQ is quickly fired up by Jack and Mike and before long we are enjoying chicken skewers, marinated in tasty herbs, along with rice, pitta breads and Greek salad. We're all sat on huge picnic blankets provided by the boat, and as drinks are handed around everyone seems in a relaxed and happy mood. Georgios is sat beside me, looking out to sea, a beer in his hand and looking pretty chilled despite his apparent inner turmoil over his novel. Chloe and Amy are sat with Jack and Mike, throwing their heads back and laughing at their jokes.

When Jack and Mike extinguish the BBQ, I notice Amy furtively take a bottle of vodka from her bag, and add a slug to her and Amy's cola and I suppress a laugh, hoping they won't regret it on the sail back later.

'Are you having a nice time?' I ask Georgios as he sits staring at a speedboat that's heading towards the small beach.

'I am, actually.' He nods slowly before taking a sip of his beer. 'Even though I'm a bit tetchy when it comes to book talk. I can't remember the last time I came out on a boat, but I used to enjoy hiring a speedboat and heading off somewhere to do some swimming and snorkelling. There are lots of small coves like this dotted about,' he informs me.

'That water does look amazing. I regret not bringing my swimming things, although my trip was pretty much last minute.' I stare at the inviting sea in front of me.

'Same here. It's a shame really, I would have liked to have gone swimming with you.' He locks eyes with me, and my face burns, which I don't think is entirely down to the effects of the sun.

'Maybe another time,' I mutter.

'I'd like that,' he says, finishing his beer as Captain Jack announces we should head back on board, and I can hardly believe how quickly the time has gone. Following Georgios up the gangplank to the boat, I stumble a little and he turns and steadies me, taking hold of my hand as he guides me onto the deck. The feel of his hand in mine is so wonderful, I don't want him to let go when we are back on terra firma.

It's been such a fantastic day, and it feels so good to have enjoyed the journey with such lovely people who are letting their hair down and enjoying every single minute of their holiday. I feel so fortunate to be able to travel. It's times like this that make me truly grateful to be alive.

Just after seven o'clock, the sun is beginning to drop as we make our sail back towards the harbour. Georgios' earlier mood at the beach has changed and I can't help noticing that he has gone into himself a little, barely joining in the conversation, so I chat to Rose, Chloe and Amy, leaving him alone with his thoughts.

After a while I begin to feel a little nauseous and regret maybe eating so much of the delicious BBQ at the beach. Sailing across the water, I can feel the rise and fall of the waves and I try to quell a feeling of sickness in the pit of my stomach. There's less chatter as the journey progresses, as most people sit quietly taking in the changing scenery. Tired-looking children are leaning against their parents, wrapped in beach towels as evening approaches, the sun turning a watery orange in the slowly darkening sky.

By the time we arrive back at the harbour and we've said goodbye to everyone, I'm really feeling ill. Amy and Chloe stay behind on board with Jack and Mike, who also invited Rose, Georgios and I below deck for drinks as it was the last sailing of the day. The three of us politely decline, leaving it as a party of four and I can see the excitement on the faces of the girls as Jack grabs a bottle of champagne from a fridge and leads them downstairs below deck.

'I have to admit I rather enjoyed that,' says Rose as she leaves us at the harbour. 'Much more than I expected to. Right, I must be off to freshen up. I'm meeting a couple of the yoga girls at the Greek Garden restaurant in the Old Town at eight thirty. You're most welcome to join us, unless you two have other plans.'

'No,' we both say at the same time.

'I mean, I think I'll have a quiet one this evening, but thanks for asking, Rose,' I say.

'And I really need to crack on with some writing,' adds Georgios.

'Are you heading back to the hotel?' I turn to Georgios.

'I am. We can walk together, if you like,' he offers.

'Sure, although do you mind if I just sit here for a few minutes.' I gesture to a bench set back from the water's edge on a patch of grass as my head swirls.

'Are you okay?' asks Georgios, when I sit down and a wave of nausea rises to the surface.

'Yes, just a little dizzy, I think. Sometimes I get a little seasick. I...'

And those were the last words I spoke before I vomited all over his blue suede shoes.

Georgios buys a bottle of water and tissues from a nearby kiosk that sells drinks and newspapers, and hands me the water, whilst he attempts to clean his shoes.

'Oh my goodness, I'm so sorry,' I say, completely mortified by what has happened. 'Maybe you could write about this in your book.' I attempt a smile, and I'm sure I see a faint smile play around Georgios' lips.

'I'm not sure it would fit in somehow,' he says.

'Oh really, what genre do you write?'

'Different genres. It depends,' he says vaguely.

'Do you want a taxi?' he asks, changing the subject as I get to my feet.

'No, it's only a short walk. The fresh air might actually do me some good.'

'You probably feel better after throwing up over my shoes.' He raises an eyebrow.

Which I realise probably cost a fortune. They are expensive-looking soft, blue suede. Probably Italian. He has managed to clean them up a bit, but even so, he seems to be taking this remarkably well.

We stroll slowly along the harbour and with every step I feel a little better, slowly sipping my water as we go. I have a slight headache, which may be down to a little dehydration, as I didn't drink much on the boat, and I guess we were out in the sunshine on the open sea. The headache brings up a memory of the first time I discovered I was ill. I'm thinking about this, once more realising how fortunate I am, when I hear a voice.

'What do you think?'

'Sorry, about what? I was miles away there.'

'I was just wondering if you wanted to grab a cold drink in the Old Town,' says Georgios.

The Old Town, with its grey and white crazy-paved streets and independent gift shops, is a short walk away, so I readily agree.

'Okay, sure. I am actually feeling a lot better now and I wouldn't mind looking around a gift shop. I'd like to get something for my friend Polly,' I tell him.

'But first, I think I need to replace my shoes.'

I wait outside while he heads into a nearby shoe shop, where he emerges a short time later wearing a pair of new loafers.

'Let me pay for them.' I take my purse from my bag, but he won't hear of it.

Ten minutes later we are sat in a pretty square, outside a restaurant with white flowers snaking over its pink-painted walls. The wooden tables are painted a light blue and terracotta pots, filled with lavender and rosemary, are lined up along the white wall. The warm breeze blowing has the plants releasing their heady scent into the early evening air.

'This is nice.' I glance around as I sip a fruit juice and pick at a few peanuts from a bowl. 'Although, I'm surprised you're not at your grandparents' place. Why don't you stay with your family?' I ask with curiosity.

'Normally I would.' He takes a sip of his cold beer. 'But not when I'm writing. My sister, her husband and my retired aunt live with my grandparents, so it can get a bit chaotic at times. Someone or other is always disturbing me. Plus, there are two noisy dogs. That's why I normally rent an apartment, or choose a small, quiet hotel.'

'Yet, still you struggle?' I find myself saying.

'Hmm.' He changes the subject by asking me some questions about myself.

'Why did you choose such a small hotel?' he asks. 'You seem to be a very sociable person from what I've seen.'

'I'd been ill,' I tell him. 'I wanted somewhere small and safe. Nothing too overwhelming. I'm only a couple of months post-surgery. One thing I was sure of though was that I wanted to return to Kos.'

I tell him about my childhood holidays here and he listens to every word. He's a very good listener, holding my gaze with his large brown eyes, nodding in the right places, frowning when a frown is needed, and smiling that delightful smile when I tell him something amusing.

'And are you better now?' he eventually asks.

'I am. I'll need check-ups in the future, but, yes. I'm lucky.'

'May I ask, did you have a serious illness? If that's not too personal a question,' he says gently.

I take a deep breath before I answer.

'I had a brain tumour.' It still feels like I'm talking about someone else, whenever I say it out loud.

He's quiet for a moment, then to my great surprise he leans across and squeezes my hand.

'And here's me worrying about putting words on paper. Your friend Rose was right. I am very lucky having the opportunity to write novels in the sunshine.' He muses. 'I am sorry for what you went through. It must have been a scary time.'

'Thanks. I won't lie, it was terrifying. But, please don't apologise. Everyone's problems are relative to their own life, I guess. Running out of salt might not be the end of the world at home, but it could spell disaster in a restaurant.'

'I like that analogy. Maybe I ought to carry a notepad around with me and write down the things people say.'

'Maybe you should. They do say truth is stranger than fiction.'

Georgios asks me more questions about my illness and how I felt during the treatment. At times, it almost feels like I am being interviewed. Maybe I am. I pull back a little, as I don't actually know what he writes about and I don't want to be the subject of his work.

Finishing our drinks, we stroll along the winding, narrow streets and I stop and look at some silver rings on display on a stand outside a shop. I spy a silver cuff bracelet with a Greek pattern that I purchase for myself, and amble around the pretty, quirky, wood-panelled shop with a large moon and stars mobile suspended from the ceiling at its centre. Its bright blue walls are covered in paintings for sale. Colourful cushions and heart-shaped lights are artfully displayed on a large sofa. It's just the kind of shop I love. I notice a pretty silver necklace with a green stone at its centre and think it would look perfect on Polly, really bringing out the colour of her eyes. As it's her birthday next month, it seems like the perfect gift so I buy that too. I'm on my way out, when I spot a notebook with a richly decorated cover, a peacock at its centre, so I add that to my purchases. I put the items in my straw bag, before heading out of the shop into the blazing sunshine once more.

We push through the crowds exploring the maze of shops selling gifts, before we discover a small outdoor market, where an assortment of lace and cotton tablecloths with a familiar olive pattern are displayed. Old ladies are sat on chairs outside the stalls, some dressed in black, and they smile as we stroll past.

'Are you hungry yet?' Georgios asks.

'Famished. My stomach is empty, remember.'

'Of course it is. How could I forget?' He laughs. 'In that case, would you like to get something to eat?'

'Didn't you say you wanted to be getting on with some work?' I remind him.

'I've decided it's a little late now, so I'm writing today off, if you'll excuse the pun.'

Georgios leads me to a café, slightly away from the main

tourist hub, that has a garden filled with shrubs and pretty white flowers in blue pots.

'If you like beef *stifado* I believe they serve the best in Kos,' he tells me.

'Even better than at your grandparents' place?' I say, surprised.

'Hmm. Maybe. My grandmother's is good, but I think her rabbit stew is her signature dish,' he admits.

We share a bottle of red wine, and I take his advice and order the beef *stifado*, the stew rich with garlic and tomatoes, served with some fluffy rice and salad. I didn't realise how hungry I was as I tuck into the tasty food.

I insist on paying the bill, but Georgios won't hear of it, so we have a bit of a disagreement about it. Eventually he reluctantly agrees to me footing the bill when I insist it's by way of an apology for the shoes.

Arriving back at the hotel, I tell Georgios how much I have enjoyed his company.

'And I'm sorry again about your shoes.' It seems I can't apologise enough.

'Don't worry about it. They're only shoes. Worse things happen at sea.' He raises an eyebrow and I laugh.

'Very funny. See you soon then. Oh, and I almost forgot.' I retrieve the notebook from my bag and hand it to Georgios outside his door. 'Maybe you can take those notes now. A small apology for the shoes.'

'But you've paid for the meal. I feel bad now, this is too much.'

'It's only a notebook.'

'And a very beautiful one. Thank you, Orla, that is so kind.' He runs his hand over the embossed cover. Our eyes meet before he leans in gently and brushes his lips against my cheek. Surprised, but pleased, I feel a blush rising. As he moves away, I can still feel his lips on my skin.

It's a little after nine as I head to my room after our walk to relax with a drink on my balcony. I am mindful not to overdo things and it has been quite a busy day, but as I open my patio door, I can hear voices down below. Peering over the balcony, the hotel residents are sitting around the pool illuminated by the lights, chatting and laughing. I am almost tempted to join them, but I need a bit of quiet time first.

Once inside, I take a shower and climb onto the top of the bed for a nap, the cool air con washing over me. As I relive the wonderful boat trip, despite the rather undignified end, and wonder what to make of Georgios, I feel my eyes go heavy and soon enough I've drifted off to sleep.

TWELVE

After a lovely nap, I open the patio door and the still warm air gushes into the room. Everyone is still gathered downstairs, and I can hear the unmistakeable voice of Brady chatting near the bar. I can also hear the tap tapping of keys on a laptop.

I glance across the balcony to Georgios, who is completely immersed in his work, so I creep back inside, happy that he seems to have found his writing mojo. After dressing, I head downstairs to join Brady and Iris around the pool area.

I take a seat around the table as Theo appears from the bar and asks if I would like a drink before he heads off out for the evening. He's dressed very smartly in dark jeans, a white shirt and a blazer over the top.

'You look very smart,' I remark as he places a beer down in front of me.

'He has a date,' says Sophia, who is lighting some candles at the centre of the long table.

'What makes you think I have a date?' he asks.

'So, you don't?'

'Maybe I do, or maybe I'm just off to a new bar in Tigaki with a few of my friends. I told you, it's Nikos' birthday.'

She smiles knowingly at her son. 'Whatever you say.'

'How was the rest of your trip?' I ask Brady and Iris. Brady is drinking cold beer and Iris has a pina colada served in a pineapple-shaped glass.

'It was just wonderful,' says Iris with a sigh.

'I'd recommend the jeep safari for sure,' adds Brady. 'Although the terrain got a little rocky in places. My backside feels as though I've spent the day on a horse.' He chuckles.

'Heck now, Brady, young Orla doesn't want to be hearing about your backside,' Iris says, slapping her husband playfully on the arm.

They tell me all about their day stopping at a mountain village and sampling some raki from a family who brew it in their own garden; they purchased some local art from a tiny gallery overlooking the mountains, and sampled delicious food at a taverna in a forest, near a lake. After that they visited a monastery and Iris said it was the most beautiful church she had ever seen. 'And to finish off, we went to a secluded beach and swam in water as clear as glass. It was like we'd arrived at the far side of paradise,' Iris finished with a sigh.

'Wow. That really does sound like a wonderful day out. Maybe I'll give it some thought.'

Even though I have a hire car, the roads they described sound like they are a little off the beaten track, so a jeep might be a better choice to explore the area.

It's almost eleven thirty when I say goodnight, taking a glass of wine to the balcony, where I think I may read for a while, not yet feeling tired after my nap earlier. Settling down with my book, I hear a voice from the next balcony.

'Good evening, Orla, how are you feeling now?' Georgios peers across the balcony, dressed in a black T-shirt and lounge pants, looking relaxed and refreshed.

'Georgios, hi. I'm as right as rain now, thanks. I'm feeling good after my siesta, so thought I'd spend a little time reading. Talking of books, did I hear you working earlier?'

'You did.' A huge smile crosses his face. 'In fact, I've managed a whole chapter since we've been back. Quite a lengthy one too.' He beams. 'Maybe being out and about has inspired me after all; there can be no inspiration locked alone with your own thoughts.'

Inspiration? I certainly hope he hasn't used any of my thoughts in his latest work of fiction.

'That's true. So, what's this particular book about then?' I ask, surprised at my own persistence, as he was very vague about his writing earlier, clearly not wanting to discuss it.

'A woman who is travelling,' he tells me.

So, he's writing about a female traveller? Surely, I'm being paranoid thinking he could be using my story as a plot line in his book. I hope I am.

'Really? I don't know why, but I would have had you down as a crime writer.'

'I have written crime novels,' he tells me. 'Several, actually. But as I said, I write in various genres. This one happens to be romantic fiction.'

'So, what happens to the main character?' I persist.

'She's inherited a crumbling villa in Spain. It's early days yet, but she's recently divorced so is making the journey alone.'

'That sounds interesting. What's your author name? Have you written anything I might have heard of?'

'Probably not. Or nothing I'd admit to writing, anyway.' He shuts down the conversation.

I lift the bottle of wine and offer him a glass. Maybe he will loosen up over a glass or two.

'Sure,' he says, then, to my surprise, he vaults over the low wall separating our two balconies and follows me inside as I go and fetch an extra wine glass. I'm suddenly aware that the room is a little messy, my clothes and hat strewn about, and my make-up bag on the coffee table. I'd intended to tidy up in the morning, not expecting any visitors. I quickly gather things up, but he doesn't seem to notice as he continues the earlier conversation.

'So, what kind of books do you prefer to read?' he asks.

'A bit of everything really. Just like you with your writing, I never stick to one genre.'

'I noticed the one you are currently reading is a Ruby King novel. Do you like her work?'

'I do, actually. Her writing is very descriptive. This one makes me long to visit the Scottish Highlands,' I tell him as I pull a glass from a shelf.

I read one book from a series she'd written years ago that I'd come across in a hotel bookcase on holiday. I recall it was set in Cornwall, and was a very enjoyable read, full of romance but with just the right amount of humour. I never did read the rest of the series though, although I did read one of her standalone books during my recovery.

'I think it's great when a writer inspires you to visit somewhere. I love it more than anything when readers reach out and tell me they've been inspired to travel to locations in my books.'

I pour him a glass of red wine and hand it to him.

'Thank you.' He looks into my eyes and gives that wonderful smile once more.

'Has Sophia mentioned the BBQ on Friday?' I ask him as we sip our wine. 'It might be a good way to get to know the other guests. Or maybe you prefer to keep yourself to yourself?'

'We'll see. If I have a good day with my writing, it might be a nice break. Will you be there?' He takes a sip of his wine.

'Most definitely. I think it's a great way to get to know people properly, especially in such a small hotel.'

We talk for a few minutes more, mainly about the resort of Kos and the lovely beaches it has to offer.

'Right, that's my break over,' says Georgios as he finishes his wine and stands up. 'I'm going to crack on while I'm in the mood.' He smiles. 'Thanks for the wine.'

'You're welcome. Goodnight, Georgios.'

I sit for a while reading but my mind is distracted by the fact that Georgios is in the room right next to me. He has such a captivating presence and I find myself hoping he will attend the BBQ evening on Friday. I can't help wondering why he is struggling to write another romance, as he's an accomplished author, although he still didn't reveal any of his works, for some reason. I googled authors with the name Georgios, but didn't find anything I could link to him, unless he's written books about house restoration.

Georgios' patio door is open, and I hear the tapping of keyboard keys once more, happy that he's back in the flow.

I'm about to head inside when I hear the sound of giggling, and see a slightly worse-for-wear-looking Amy and Chloe walking across the pool area towards the bar.

'Aw it's closed,' moans Amy, who is walking in a way that suggests she has already had more than enough.

'Never mind. We've got that bottle of sambuca in our room.'

'Ooh yeah,' Amy replies with a giggle, then she suddenly glances up at my balcony and waves.

'Unless you feel like going out for a dance? The night is still young.'

'Yeeah! Let's go. Fancy joining us, Orla?' Amy calls up to me.

'Maybe another night, thanks, girls, I'm heading to bed shortly.'

'Sure. See you tomorrow then.' They link arms and disappear out of the gate into the town centre and I'd put money on them missing breakfast in the morning.

THIRTEEN

The next morning I'm surprised to see Georgios at the breakfast table. It's the second morning of all our stays, and yet it's the first time Iris and Brady have met him. After introductions are made, we load our plates up with the tempting-looking buffet. This morning there is delicious brown granary bread for toasting, smashed avocados, hummus and fat juicy tomatoes, along with the usual meats, cheeses and yoghurts. There is also a delicious-looking lemon cake that Sophia told me she had made with lemons from the trees surrounding the pool.

'Cake for breakfast, I think that's something I could get used to.' I place a slice of cake onto a small plate.

'Lots of European countries have cake on the breakfast buffet. I guess it's the best time to eat it,' says Brady, helping himself to a generous slice.

I thought as most of you aren't around in the afternoon, I would serve it at breakfast.' Sophia explains. 'Oh and if any of you fancy pancakes, I have a jug of some mixture and some rather nice honey. Blueberries too,' she announces as she tops up everyone's coffee from a pot. This morning she's wearing a blue wrap dress, her hair tied back and immaculately applied make-up. She looks as though she might be off out for the day, rather than spending time in the kitchen cooking pancakes.

'Theo will make the pancakes. I have a meeting this morning with the bank.' Which explains the nice dress. 'Enjoy your breakfast, everyone, and have a nice day.' She blows kisses to us all, then dashes off.

Right on cue, Theo appears from the kitchen, yawning, his hair slightly messy, and looking exhausted.

'Are you sure you don't need a hand in the kitchen?' I offer when he passes the table, stifling another yawn.

'No, I'll be fine. I do not expect the guests to help, you are here on holiday. Can I get anyone pancakes?' he says, half-heartedly.

Brady eagerly accepts, whilst Georgios and I stick to the cold buffet on offer. Theo is about to head back to the kitchen when Chloe and Amy join us.

'Ooh did I hear someone mention pancakes? Yes, please,' says Amy. They both, surprisingly, look as fresh as a daisy, wearing shorts, T-shirts and fake designer sunglasses, that look very like the genuine article. Chloe told me the day of the pirate sail that they'd purchased the glasses for eight euros from a shop on the harbour front and urged me to buy some.

Fifteen minutes later, Theo appears with a plate piled high with delicious-looking pancakes. Along with a basket of blueberries and a jar of mountain honey.

'Any Nutella?' asks Choe, helping herself to a pancake.

'No,' says Theo bluntly, before adding, 'Sorry, it's not something that is usually requested.'

'You look as rough as that toast this morning,' says Amy cheekily to Theo, pointing to Brady's toast. 'I thought I would be too but I actually feel fine. I think all that dancing helped.' She laughs, before downing a glass of fresh orange juice.

Theo smiles weakly, before checking no one needs anything else, then disappears.

Over breakfast, talk turns to careers, and Brady asks Georgios what he does for a living.

'I'm in publishing,' he says vaguely.

'You're not an editor, are you?' asks Chloe, her ears pricking up. ''Cos I wrote a book once.' She helps herself to another pancake and slathers it with honey and berries.

'Did you?' Amy looks stunned.

'Yeah. It's in the bottom drawer in my bedroom back home. I wrote it when I was about nineteen, I think.'

'What type of book is it?' asks Georgios, after telling her that no, he isn't an editor and luckily for him she doesn't probe any further.

'A crime thriller about a bloke who'd been murdered by his ex-girlfriend. I'd been dumped by someone just after Christmas, so it gave me the inspiration. I was fuming.' She shakes her head as she cuts into her pancake with a knife. 'I'd spent a bloody fortune on his Christmas present.'

Amy bursts out laughing. The rest of us are unsure whether we ought to laugh along or not.

'Oh, don't worry, it was five years ago, I can laugh about it now. I think the story is quite good though,' she says confidently.

'Maybe you should try finding an agent,' says Georgios as he sips a coffee.

'I have thought about it once or twice. Do you think your publishers might like to take a look?' she asks.

'I'm afraid most publishers won't look at new submissions without an agent these days.' He shifts in his seat. 'Although you should take a look online. Good luck.' He glances at his watch. 'Goodness, is that the time, I must be off, I have work to do.'

'I thought you were here on holiday?' says Iris, who's looking lovely today in a blue-patterned kaftan and a clip with a fake blue flower in her hair.

'It's true, but I'm going to see my family at Neptune's restaurant this morning to help out a little. I recommend it, by the way. It's a great restaurant.'

'I can vouch for that,' I chime in, as I recall the delicious meal I had when I first arrived here.

'Your English is amazing. You are Greek, aren't you?' Amy asks.

'Born and bred in London. But I have a Greek father and English mother.'

Looking at Georgios' complexion, and dark hair and eyes, it's hard to believe both of his parents are not from Greece.

He pushes his chair back and tells Brady and Iris what a pleasure it was to meet them, before leaving, barely making eye contact with me this morning, despite the time we spent in the Old Town yesterday after the pirate ship and the drink on my balcony. What is it with this guy?

'Oh my gosh, he really is gorgeous, isn't he?' says Chloe, watching him as he leaves. 'Is he in the room next to yours?' she asks.

'He is. I don't see a lot of him though.' I almost say because he's busy writing, before I stop myself. I can't help wondering whether he really has agreed to help out in the family restaurant today, or whether he will lock himself away and carry on working on his novel. I get the feeling he has just complicated things by not being completely honest about his true identity though. And I'm not entirely sure it's fair of him, asking me to keep it quiet and lie to these kind people for him. But it's not my secret to keep.

I have no time to dwell on this though, as today I have decided to take a drive to the Asklepion to take in a little culture, so after breakfast I head upstairs to grab my bag and straw hat and head off.

I'm driving along the coast road again, passing the same shops, bars and cafés already full with diners at outside tables, eating their breakfast as the sun blazes down, signalling another beautiful day. Approaching a zebra crossing, I spot Rose walking along, looking stylish in a white jumpsuit, sleeves pushed up to her elbows, large straw hat and a designer bag flung over her shoulder.

'Rose.' I wind my window down and say hi as a throng of people make their way over the crossing.

'Orla, hi. Where are you off to?' she asks.

'I'm heading to the Asklepion for a wander about before the sun really gets up; how about you?'

'No plans really, a bit of shopping, maybe a swim later,' she says vaguely.

'Do you fancy joining me?' I offer.

'Sure! I'd love to.'

She climbs into the passenger seat, and when the crowd have finally finished crossing the road, we head off.

'Are you enjoying your holiday?' she asks, taking a compact from her bag and refreshing her lipstick as we drive.

'I really am. It's so lovely to be here, as I have some nice memories from my childhood holidays in Kos. I'll be moving on to Patmos after here, which is somewhere I haven't been to before.'

I'm looking forward to going to Patmos, rich in history and religion, even though my reason for doing so gives me a knotted feeling in my stomach when I think about it. It's where a meeting may change my life after all.

'How exciting. Are you island hopping then?'

'Kind of. From Patmos I'll maybe head to Samos, then I'll probably sail to Rhodes where I will fly back home. I'm not certain yet though. I have a habit of changing my mind about things.'

I feel so grateful to be able to do these things and fully embrace life. The alternative doesn't even bear thinking about.

'And how is the delectable Georgios?' she asks, casting a sideways glance at me, catching the smile on my face.

'He seems fine. He's actually getting some words down on paper. He's an author, as you are aware, but he doesn't want people to know for some reason.'

'I can understand that. Imagine constantly being asked how the book is going, what's the plot etc. I can imagine how annoying that would be. Maybe it's just because he's stressed and up against a deadline. I'm sure he doesn't keep it a secret if he meets someone socially.'

'No, maybe not,' I say, although I'm not sure about anything when it comes to Georgios.

'And how is Theo?' she asks.

'He looked exhausted this morning. Just as well he doesn't have a yoga class until tomorrow.' I laugh. 'He could barely keep his eyes open at breakfast.'

'I had a late night too. I bumped into Theo last night, actually,' she tells me. 'He was out with a group of friends, celebrating someone's birthday.' A slow smile spreads across her face. 'His friends headed off to a nightclub and we had a drink at a late bar I know, near my apartment,' she reveals.

'You and Theo?' My surprise surely shows on my face.

'Don't look so shocked. I've known Theo a little while, he's a darling. It was only a bit of fun, nothing more.'

'I'm not shocked, just surprised. Given your determination to try and stay on the wagon, as it were.'

'I know, but when I'm around Theo, it's just so hard.'

'I bet it is. For him anyway.'

Rose roars with laughter.

Rose is a very attractive lady, with a body that would be the envy of a woman half her age, which is still indeterminate – today she looks about thirty-five.

'Well, you look good on it,' I remark.

'Thanks. And while we're talking of men, I take it you know that Georgios likes you, don't you?'

'Likes me? How would you know that?'

'Yesterday on the pirate ship. I saw the glances he was casting your way. I'd say he looked quite smitten.'

I turn to look at her. 'Smitten? Really? I'd say he was more absorbed with thinking about his latest novel.'

Thinking about it though, I probably never noticed, as I was concentrating hard on not throwing up. Especially on the sail back to the harbour.

'I know what I saw. And who can blame him. You're gorgeous. You look just like a young Debbie Harry. Please tell me you know who she is, or I'll feel ancient?' She laughs.

'Of course I know who Debbie Harry is. And you flatter me.'

I glance in the mirror at my tousled silver, lightly streaked hair and pink lips. Maybe I have a similar look, and thinking about it, my eyes are probably the same shape and colour. Debbie Harry from Blondie – I'll definitely take that.

Driving away from the harbour, we head into the mountain roads and are soon surrounded by olive groves, following dusty single-track roads that make me wish I'd hired a jeep rather than a Citroën, but we manage the terrain somehow.

Stepping out of the car into the searing heat, I glance out at the ruins in front of us, eager to explore and wishing I had brought a camera with me, although I do have the one on my phone. I have noticed that Chloe carries a rather expensive-looking Nikon camera with her for her holiday snaps and wish I had one too.

Before we look around, we stop for a drink at a little outdoor café close by, shaded by huge trees.

'I never did ask you,' I say to Rose as we sip a refreshing iced peach tea. 'What is it you do for a living?'

'Would you believe me if I told you I was a therapist? Not a sex therapist, obviously.' She holds a cigarette up before grabbing an ashtray from a nearby table.

'You're a smoking therapist.' I laugh.

'I know. Can you imagine? I feel like such a hypocrite.' She lights up and blows a plume of smoke into the air. 'Although I have really cut down, less than five a day. From twenty,' she tells me.

'Well done. That can't have been easy.'

'It wasn't. And I must admit, rightly or wrongly, I tell my clients to cut down too, if they really can't quit. I'll stop eventually,' she says positively. 'I like holding a cigarette though. Maybe I'll get one of those fake ones that light up red at the end. We used to get them as kids from the joke shop and horrify our parents.' She laughs. 'Oh gosh, I'm giving my age away again, aren't I?' she says, probably noticing my blank expression.

'I do hypnotherapy on some people. I'm a trained hypnotherapist,' she tells me.

'Really? How interesting. Maybe you could hypnotise me into staying in one place for more than five minutes.'

'Have you always been that way?' she asks with interest.

'Not always, I had a bunch of friends as a child at school and a best friend called Lynsey on the street I grew up on. As I got older though I grew restless and even though I made friends easily I could never really sustain friendships, as I liked to go off on my own a lot. My mum said it all started when my teenage hormones kicked in. And I think she's probably right,' I confess. 'It seems friends need input like everything else in life and I've realised I'm just not very good at it.'

'What about relationships?' she asks and I half expect her to take a pen and a notebook from her bag as she psychoanalyses me.

'The same, I suppose. Don't get me wrong, I've been in love.

At least I think I have. Maybe it was just a teenage crush. But when it comes to putting down roots, I just panic.'

'It could be that you haven't met the one you want to settle down with. It might be as simple as that.' She takes a drag of her cigarette.

'I just get bored so quickly and feel hemmed in when someone suggests living together. I never know what I want to do from one day to the next. I'm surprised I've stayed so long in my job at Potters, to be honest. Although I just feel closer to the people there then I have anywhere I've ever worked.'

I tell her all about the job I do back home and my colleagues.

'I am close to Polly though. But not enough to stop me from travelling, if that doesn't sound too awful.'

'I don't think so. You are who you are. Do you have any siblings?' she asks.

'No, actually, I'm an only child,' I reply, not wanting to discuss my discovery with Rose right now. Not when I'm still unsure of the truth.

'Maybe you see your colleagues as a substitute family. Did you dislike being an only child?' she asks bluntly.

I feel an unexpected pang of regret as I think about her question.

'Maybe I did. I had the most beautiful doll's house, filled with tiny people. They were my own little family,' I tell her, smiling at the memory of the pretty red-roofed house. 'Do you have children?' I ask, in an attempt to move the discussion away from me.

'Yes, a son, Ash. He's twenty and at university studying to be an architect. He's a good son, and I him see regularly, but I never felt the desire to have any more children,' she tells me honestly.

We finish our drinks and head towards the entrance to the site, where we pay a fee and enter the ruins of the Asklepion. It feels quite haunting treading the path of what was once an ancient hospital on the ground floor. Asclepius was a doctor who founded this hospital, which is such a beautiful building, and worked with the famous Hippocrates who created the Hippocratic oath, still observed by doctors today.

I think about Rose's comments as we wander through the gardens, admiring the flowers and looking up at intricately carved masonry above heavy oak doors. Could I fear settling down simply because I haven't found the love of my life? Do I fear settling down? Especially after my cancer treatment? There are times when I still fear it will return, so perhaps I subconsciously worry about becoming a mother and leaving a child alone. If I did have a family, I would like to have more than one child, and wonder if it is even possible after my cancer treatment. Rose made me face the fact that my childhood was lonely, despite my parents doing their very best to keep me entertained, which must have been difficult for them at times. And something I have recently learned of fills my head with a thousand different emotions.

I try to shake these thoughts off as we explore the ruins, determined to enjoy the glorious day in such stunning surroundings.

'Oh wow, just look at this view,' says Rose.

From its slightly elevated position, the hospital gives a stunning view of the sea below through the branches of the trees. I imagine patients sitting on the beaches here recuperating and admiring the vista below.

'It's wonderful, isn't it? What a lovely place to have a hospital, if you see what I mean.'

It's hard to believe that some of the structures are still intact, despite them being built thousands of years ago. One or two pillars have fallen across the ground, others standing upright defying the time and elements. There's a crumbling staircase that would have led to the upper floor of the hospital. I snap away with my phone camera, vowing to print some of the photographs when I get home and maybe make a collage of Kos to display on a wall. The sun is beating down as we wander amongst the crumbling ruins, stopping to read information boards. A family are walking around with a bored-looking teenage boy in tow, staring at his phone.

'Maybe one day you will appreciate history,' I hear his father say, and he replies, 'Yeah, when I'm, like, a hundred years old myself,' before his gaze returns to his phone.

'Look at this, Rose.' I show her a room that looks surprisingly intact with most of the floor and the clear remains of a wall.

'Amazing, isn't it? I guess some things are just made to last.'

An hour later, having marvelled at the ancient remains, we drive a little further along and find a restaurant high up in the hills. It's very basic, with wooden tables covered with paper cloths, no plants in pots, or music playing adding to the usual ambience. A dog is resting on a porch, which is the entrance to the restaurant. An elderly man greets us with a smile, and we take a seat on one of five exterior tables, three of which are occupied. The view here is of mountains, olive groves and a distant white church on the hillside. The menu consists of a Greek salad, lamb and butter bean stew, or chicken souvlaki with rice.

After ordering some cold drinks, we both opt for the lamb and butter bean stew. The elderly grey-haired man smiles, and tells us, 'Good choose.' I think he means good choice, his English limited.

'So, what's next?' asks Rose as she sips a glass of chilled wine, while I opt for a tall glass of cola filled with ice and a slice of lemon.

'I'm thinking a swim in the hotel pool later, then maybe a little stroll around the local shops.'

'I could sit here all day, it's just so beautiful.' Rose sighs, casting her eyes around our surroundings. 'Kos has so many attractions.'

'Like Theo?' I tease.

'There is no doubting his physical attributes, but I wasn't thinking of Theo.' She smiles. 'Last night was a drunken one-off, which, if I'm honest, I already regret. I've been coming to Kos for a few years, and have known Theo since then. We first met on the beach at one of his yoga classes. I like to think we are friends. I hope he won't be embarrassed at our next session.'

'Of yoga?' I raise an eyebrow.

'Yes! Of yoga, cheeky.'

'I'm sure he won't be. He's a young, single man enjoying his life. He probably knows you're not expecting marriage. You're not, are you?' I tease.

'Will you stop. Of course not! You do make me smile, Orla, I'm glad I ran into you.'

'I'm glad too.'

A short while later, a tasty aroma wafts towards our table, as the elderly gentleman carries a tray with two deep, white bowls filled with a delicious stew. He places some bread in a wooden basket also on the table.

'*Efcharisto.*'

'Oh, I can't wait to dive into this, I'm starved,' I say, before taking a large mouthful of the tastiest stew I think I've ever eaten. The lamb is beautifully tender, and the juicy tomato sauce is rich with herbs, olives and soft butter beans.

'I love these little rustic places in the mountains,' says Rose. 'The simple, home-made food is just wonderful. I'm glad chips aren't on the menu though. I have trouble resisting them.' She dips a chunk of home-made bread into the stew, and makes an appreciative noise as she chews it.

'I wish I could resist them too. My dad still makes them, although only once a week. He has fish and chips like he has done for years, every Friday, the chips cooked in a proper chip pan. I bought him an Actifryer that's still sitting in its box in a cupboard.'

'Old habits die hard, I guess, although I believe everything is okay in moderation. Once a week, home-made fish and chips sounds just wonderful.'

'Well, if you're ever in the North of England, you could join us for Fish Friday, you'd be more than welcome.'

I do mean it, but find myself wondering how many people actually look each other up, once a holiday has ended. Often once the holiday is over, we usually remember the people we met with little more than a fond smile when we browse our photos.

We finish our delicious meal, enjoying the stunning surroundings, before finishing with a frappé and leaving a generous tip. The drive along the mountainous road, surrounded by lush scenery, is wonderful, and I drive slowly taking it all in. I wind the window down so I can feel a breeze ruffle my hair as I drive. It feels so free and relaxing here, I really wish I could stay in this moment forever.

'I enjoyed today,' says Rose when I drop her off outside the apartment she is renting. 'Maybe I will see you at yoga in the morning?'

'Ooh definitely. I'll look forward to it. See you there,' I say, recalling the last time I went, and how wonderful it felt, waking to the rising sun on the serene beach at such an early hour.

I park up and head to my room, once again hearing Georgios working on his computer outside and tapping away at the keyboard, as I slide the patio door open. I change into my swimwear and take a long, relaxing swim in the pool, which I have all to myself because the rest of the guests appear to be out for the day. Returning to my room a while later, I grab my book and quietly head outside to the balcony to read, not wishing to disturb Georgios. Ten minutes into my book, I hear Georgios' voice.

'Orla, hi, how's things?'

Georgios is smiling broadly, in a seemingly great mood. I just can't figure him out though.

'Hi, Georgios. I didn't want to disturb you. I take it the writing is going well?'

'I think it is,' he tells me, sounding positive. 'I spent half the night working, had some breakfast, then started again a few hours ago. It's going really well, actually.'

'Haven't you slept?' I'm surprised he's managed to power on all night, and still look fresh. Not to mention gorgeous.

'I managed a couple of hours. I was fuelled by lots of coffee. I'm fine.' He smiles.

He's wearing a blue linen shirt, sleeves rolled up and beige shorts. Around his neck he's wearing a leather necklace with a silver cross, his slightly damp hair is slicked back and he smells as if he has just stepped out of the shower.

'I'm pleased it's going well. Dare I ask what it's about?' Worth a try, I think, as I place my book down on the table.

'I still don't have an exact plot; let's just say it's kind of evolving,' he says vaguely.

'So, you don't have the story worked out, before you write it?' I ask with interest.

'I never do. Obviously I have a vague plot somewhere in my head, but I like to see how the story evolves and go where the characters take me,' he reveals. 'Life doesn't always turn out the way we plan, does it? I like my art to imitate life a little. Although, of course, the ending is always perfectly tied up and they live happily ever after, which doesn't always happen in real life.' His expression looks serious for a split second.

'That's what the reader wants though. The fact that things

do turn out exactly the way they are meant to. Boy meets girl, they fall in love and get their happy ever after.'

'Is that what people expect in real life?' he says. 'Is it what you hope for too?'

'Maybe. I never expect anything. I kind of just like to see what turns up. A bit like you really.'

Georgios glances at his watch. 'If you'll excuse me, I'm running an errand for my grandfather shortly. I probably need a break from my laptop anyway, but I was wondering, would you care to join me for dinner this evening?'

'At your grandparents' place?' I remember how much I enjoyed the quirky interior, and the ambience there.

'I was thinking of somewhere a little smaller, to be honest. A place I know, close to the beach, but we can go to Neptune's if you really like it so much,' he offers.

'No, not at all. A beach restaurant sounds lovely, I'd like that, thanks.'

In fact, I think having dinner on the beach, with the sound of waves rolling in the background, sounds very intimate. I would like that very much.

'Great, shall we say, seven thirty?'

'Sounds good. See you later then.'

Georgios heads off, and I return to my book, thinking about the author and wondering whether they experienced any writer's block. If they did, they certainly got over it as it's the most wonderful, sweeping tale of love and loss. It's mesmerising and a real page-turner. I've never been to a remote Scottish castle as described in the book, although I have visited Edinburgh Castle when I went there for a weekend with Mum and Dad as a teenager.

Around five o'clock, I head downstairs to the pool area as Chloe and Amy are returning from the beach, walking sand from their flip-flops onto the tiled floor, as Sophia walks behind them, sweeping, always sure to keep the area clean. She follows us to the bar, propping her brush behind it.

'*Kalispera*, ladies. I hope you have enjoyed your day?' she asks, before asking us if we would like a drink. I order a glass of white wine as Amy and Chloe opt for a cold beer, and then tell her all about my day at the Asklepion.

'It's so wonderful there, isn't it?' says Sophia. 'A reminder of how lucky we are to have such wonderful doctors. Medical research has saved so many lives,' she ponders.

'That's so true.' I think of the wonderful doctor who did the surgery on my tumour. Realising I would almost certainly have died a hundred years ago.

'Oh, and I am heading to a market in the morning for Friday night's BBQ so I will need numbers. I know Orla, Brady and Iris are coming, but how about you guys?'

'What time?' asks Chloe as she sips her beer.

'Seven thirty.'

'Great we'll be there, won't we?' She turns to Amy, who nods.

'Yeah, sure. We'll probably go clubbing later, so it's probably best to get some food inside of us.'

'Wonderful. I just need to ask Georgios if he is attending,' says Sophia, who is dressed in green cotton trousers and a white blouse, and seems to look younger with every day that passes. After serving our drinks, she bustles about emptying ashtrays and wiping tables that don't really need wiping, singing as she goes.

'You're in a cheerful mood,' I can't help remarking.

'Am I? Yes, maybe I am.' She smiles, taking a seat beside me on a wicker chair. 'I have exciting plans for the hotel,' she reveals. 'I went to my bank this morning and they have agreed to a loan for an extension. I am going to have two more bedrooms.' She can barely keep the excitement from her voice.

'I take it that's great news for you?'

'It is. It's something I have wanted for a long time. Business has been going so well lately, I'm lucky enough to have lots of return visitors, so the bank has agreed the loan.'

She tells me they will build into the car park, which is too large for the number of rooms currently in use. 'And it will keep any old Tom, Dick and Henry from parking there, even though I have a sign on the wall that says for residents of the hotel only.'

'Harry.'

'Harry who?'

'People usually say, Tom, Dick and Harry, that's all.' I laugh.

'Ah, I see. Oh well, Henry, Harry, I couldn't remember. Although, I knew there was a Dick in there somewhere,' she says and has us all laughing.

We sip our drinks and the girls tell me they have been waterskiing on the beach at Tigaki.

'Oh my gosh, you should come next time,' says Chloe. 'It was amazing. I've never done it before. It was such a blast. Well, apart from one small mishap.' She pulls a face.

Amy almost chokes in her drink as she speaks. 'Don't start me off laughing again, I've only just recovered. Topless water-skiing is more than a small mishap, Chloe.' She laughs loudly.

'What?' I look from Amy to Chloe open-mouthed.

'Things went a little wrong as I obviously hadn't fastened my bikini top properly, that's all,' she tells me as Amy struggles to contain her giggles.

'It was okay at first but when the boat got some speed up' – she pauses for dramatic effect – 'my bikini top flew off.'

'It never!' My hand flies to my mouth.

'Oh, it did,' she continues. 'It flew into the air like a red kite before landing in the face of one of the jet-skiers.' Amy's creasing up again as Chloe continues the story. 'The blokes on the jet-skis got a right eyeful. I was trying to hold on to the ski handle with one hand and cover my boobs with the other.'

'Luckily, one of the jet-ski guys got the attention of our boat driver, who slowed down so he could return the top to Chloe.'

'Well, I am never going to that beach again, which is a shame as I like it there,' says Chloe.

'Oh, I don't know,' says Amy. 'We might bump into those fit jet-skiers again. They might have liked what they saw.' She chuckles.

Chloe thumps Amy on the arm before bursting into laughter. 'I can laugh about it now, I suppose,' she concedes. 'But I wanted to die at the time.'

'That's one holiday memory you won't forget in a hurry,' I say, recalling my own holiday horror, when I once stripped off on a nudist beach in Ibiza that was deserted at the time. I woke half an hour later to a lady in a swimming costume telling me that the nudist beach was at a cove further along. It had been towards the end of the first week of a two-week holiday, with my then boyfriend, when I decided I wanted to spend some time alone. He wondered why, as he said he'd expected us to spend every minute together on holiday and we'd argued. I took myself off to the secluded beach, wondering how someone could feel offended by their partner wanting to have some alone time. Don't we all need time to gather our thoughts and connect with ourselves? Not for the first time, I wonder if it's me who thinks differently to other people. Maybe I really am better off alone.

'Have you been sunbathing today?' asks Chloe. 'You have a lovely tan now,' she remarks.

'Thanks. I've actually caught a lot of this walking around the Asklepion today, with Rose.'

'Is that the old hospital ruins? Oh, it's gorgeous, isn't it?' says Amy. 'I really imagine the people walking around there, thousands of years ago. Such an important place, as I believe it was the first ever hospital in the world,' she says knowledgeably. 'I also love the Roman villa,' she continues. 'It's the sense of atmosphere in those places that I love.'

'Me too.' I agree. 'It also reminds me that however important we think we are, our time on earth is fleeting. Chloe, you would get some great photos there.'

'That sounds amazing. I might actually head over there with my camera one day before we leave,' says Chloe.

I'm slightly ashamed to admit that I never had Amy down as a history lover. She tells me she is a second-year student studying history, but likes to let her hair down on holiday.

'I flunked my A-levels first time, 'cos I couldn't be arsed doing any studying,' she tells me honestly as we chat about our respective careers. 'I was more interested in an instant income, but two years in a dead-end job made me realise I didn't want it for the rest of my life. So, I went back to night school to do my A-levels, with a totally different mindset, and here we are. I think I'm actually mature enough to appreciate my education now at the grand old age of twenty-five.'

'Good for you. It's so hard to make decisions about your future when you're so young, isn't it?'

'Tell me about it,' says Amy, so I do. I tell them all about my jobs, including the stint in the circus and they can hardly believe their ears.

'You actually joined a circus?' says Chloe, open-mouthed. 'I always fancied doing something like that, but the wildest thing I've ever done was to dress up like a chicken and hand out leaflets for the fast-food chicken shop in the town centre.' She laughs at the memory. 'These days I work in the chicken shop, minus the outfit, whilst I'm at uni studying photography. It's where me and Amy met two years ago.'

Which explains the smart camera she carries around with her during daytime hours.

'I imagined you had an interest in photography when I noticed your camera.'

'A present from my parents. I think they are hoping it will

persuade me to stay at uni. I will though, as I'm really enjoying it.'

I wonder whether I might consider a career change when I get home, much as I love my Potters family, who I have no doubt I would keep in touch with. Money isn't a consideration, after all, so maybe it's time to develop some new skills, maybe attending art college to develop my drawing. Or perhaps that will remain strictly a hobby, and I will train to be a nurse and work in geriatrics. I've always loved old people; I find their stories so enriching and interesting. It makes me feel good to know that there are so many possibilities for me to explore and I find Amy and Chloe really inspiring.

A while later, a glance at my watch tells me its six o'clock, so I head to my room to get ready for my date with Georgios. I find myself feeling a tiny bit excited at the thought of our meeting, but push those feelings away as I will be moving on in a few days' time. Even so, it will be nice to spend the evening in the company of a man I find beguiling and attractive.

I choose a black vest accessorised with a silver heart necklace, and a long pink skirt that matches my lipstick. A squirt of Alien, which is my go-to evening perfume, and I'm ready to go.

I've just finished applying a winged eyeliner when there's a tap on my bedroom door and I open it to the sight of Georgios holding a bunch of red roses.

'Hi.' I feel almost a little shy, standing here in front of him.

'Good evening.' He hands me the roses and I thank him.

'Wow, they are beautiful, thank you.'

'You're welcome. And may I say, you look particularly lovely this evening.'

'You may indeed. And so do you.'

He looks effortlessly sexy, in a black shirt and grey jeans, his shoulder-length hair tied back. The smell of his aftershave is delightfully woody without being overpowering.

'So how was your day?' I ask as we head down the stairs.

'Good. My sister had me help her move house, shifting some furniture about as her partner has broken his arm. She's always abusing my good nature,' he tells me, half smiling.

'So, you didn't take it as a reason to procrastinate?'

'Are you kidding? I'm in the zone now, I've actually written quite a few chapters,' he reveals. 'But when family need help, they need help.'

'Do your parents live here too?' I ask.

'No, they actually live in England. My grandparents hoped they would settle in Greece one day, but they made a life in London. My father actually runs a very successful Greek restaurant there. I kind of live in both places.'

'Lucky you. Do you actually live in London?'

'Yes, I have an apartment not far from my parents' restaurant in Camden Town. How about you?'

'I live in Cheshire.'

'Very nice. Isn't it full of expensive houses and swanky restaurants?'

'Not all of it, although some areas, yes, especially Alderley Edge, which is home to millionaire businessmen and Premiership footballers. I live in Knutsford, which is also very nice. I rent an apartment there.'

I realise I should probably buy an apartment, now that I have the money to do so. Dad is probably right about having some security for the future, as given my lust for travel, the money won't last forever.

FOURTEEN

'Does your sister live here?' I ask him as we turn towards the rear of the hotel to the car park.

'Yes, she settled here and married a Greek, much to the delight of my grandparents. They did the whole Greek wedding thing, at the restaurant when the season was over. The party went on for days,' he recalls, smiling. 'And even though it was early November, the sun shone. My grandmother said they had been blessed by the Greek gods.'

'What do your parents think of your sister living in Greece?' I ask.

'They're fine with it now. She visits home a lot, she is a good daughter, and, of course, they come here, though maybe not as much as they would like to with the commitment of the restaurant. Sometimes they think of selling up and retiring, but if they are anything like my grandparents, I can't see it happening anytime soon. My grandmother is eighty-two and still cooks in the kitchen.'

'That's pretty impressive.'

'It is, although sometimes she is a little forgetful. These days, I think she is under the watchful eye of my sister and the other chefs,' he adds. 'The restaurant has grown so much over the years, it's very popular.'

I can't help thinking that it sounds like the perfect life, spending time in both countries, escaping a rainy spell in England, to be bathing in sunshine several hours later. Maybe a holiday home is something I ought to consider buying.

I'm surprised we are going out in a car because when he suggested a beach restaurant, I assumed he meant something local. Arriving at the car park, Georgios points his key at a smart blue Mercedes to unlock it. It looks slightly out of place, alongside the other small cars, including my hire car.

'Nice car,' I remark.

'Thank you. I leave it here in Kos, as I travel back and forth so much. It's an older model, but I like to look after things that mean a lot to me.' His eyes meet mine and for some reason I feel my cheeks colour.

'So, what have you been up to today?' he asks as we drive along the palm tree avenue on the harbour. I recount my day as we drive through the archway alongside the castle and head slightly out of town. Fifteen minutes later, we are approaching Tigaki, the sparkling sea gently rolling beneath the orange sun that is beginning to drop, leaving empty sunbeds beneath the straw sunshades on the beach.

Parking up, Georgios leads me to a restaurant at the far end of the beach, where Greek music is gently playing in the background. Several couples are seated outside at tables on a wooden terrace, candles lit in storm glasses decorating the tables. The location looks like just the place for a romantic liaison, and I can't help wondering why he has chosen such a place.

We take a seat and are soon sat enjoying a cold beer each in the balmy evening.

'It's beautiful here, isn't it?' I take a sip of my drink and glance across the water, the sound of the sea gradually becoming louder as the sky darkens and silvery stars appear. 'It must be hard returning to England, especially in the summer months.'

'Sometimes it is, although I like the change of scenery. And, of course, I like to see my parents.'

'Do you enjoy travelling?' I ask.

'I visit the locations in my books, so, yes, I guess I do. Italy is a particular favourite of mine. Have you ever been there?' he asks.

'Only through a book I once read. I think it was called *One Night in Naples*. In fact, I think it was the other Ruby King novel I read, whilst recuperating.'

'Did you enjoy it?'

'Honestly? I really did. In fact, it was wonderful. It really took me out of myself. I always intended to read more of her books, but honestly, it's a genre I only dip into occasionally.'

'I'm glad you liked it. To tell you the truth, it was one of my favourites too.'

'You read Ruby King novels?' I ask, a little surprised.

He takes another sip of his beer before he locks eyes with me.

'I do. In fact' – he pauses for a few seconds – 'maybe it's because I am Ruby King.'

'What?' I almost spit my drink all over the table. 'You're Ruby King? Are you winding me up?'

'Nope, it's me. I've written under that pseudonym for a long time in the romantic genre. Lots of blokes write women's romance.'

'I guess so, but, wow, you're Ruby King? I can't believe it!'

Some evenings, Polly would call around and read a few chapters of *One Night in Naples*, when I grew tired and was in danger of overdoing things, the pair of us giggling at the sex scenes, which were quite raunchy. Wait until I tell her that I've had dinner with the author, Ruby King. Suddenly I'm thinking of the amorous antics of the heroine in her apartment overlooking the sea. Who would have thought it was written by this handsome, but very moody, man.

'What about you?'

'Sorry? I was miles away there.' I daren't tell him what I was thinking about.

'I was just asking have you travelled much?'

I tell him about the places I visited after I became ill, whilst still trying to process the fact that Ruby King is the alter ego of Georgios.

'I particularly loved Paris. I regret not seeing a show at the Moulin Rouge though. I know it's touristy, but I really fancied the old-fashioned music hall glamour of it all. I think I was inspired to visit after watching the movie with Ewan McGregor. I was travelling alone at the time and would have felt a bit self-conscious going in there on my own.'

'You went to the city of love alone?' He smiles.

'I did. But I quite like travelling alone. You'd be surprised how brave you become after you've survived a brain tumour.'

Which, I realise, is probably why I'm pursuing something I would never have had the courage to do in the past.

'I can only imagine,' he says sincerely. 'Although you never seem to be alone for long, so I guess you are a people person at heart.'

'I suppose I am, yes.'

Our food arrives, which is a sharing meze and includes aubergine dips, stuffed vine leaves and crispy deep-fried whitebait. There are meatballs in a rich tomato sauce, balsamic and olive oil for dipping pitta bread. After a second glass of wine, my mood is mellow and as I stare at Georgios' face bathed in candlelight across the table, I feel a warm glow. He has the face of a Greek god and I'm finding I'm enjoying spending time with him more and more.

'Talking of travelling,' I tell him as I dip some bread into the sensational aubergine dip. 'I'll be moving on to Patmos in a few days.'

'Patmos, really? You know it's very quiet there. Although not at this time of year, it will have hordes of pilgrims who travel there to visit the holy cave,' he tells me.

'I'd actually read about that, yes. Isn't it where John the Apostle is said to have written the Book of Revelation?'

'That's right. Whether he actually wrote the scripture in the cave is a little unproven. But he definitely visited Patmos. It's written in the Bible.'

'How interesting.' And religious monuments aside, I think it sounds like such a change from Kos, rugged and unspoilt. I'm looking forward to spending some quiet time, just walking and reading. Maybe a little swimming. And looking someone up.

I sip my wine, captivated by the wonderful surroundings, but mainly by the company.

'It is said that a vision appeared before his eyes, instructing him to write the words describing the final days of Armageddon as written in the Book of Revelation. Christians flock there at certain times of the year.'

I'm thinking that maybe it won't be as quiet as I had hoped, but it sounds like an interesting place to visit all the same.

'So where will you be heading after Patmos?' He twirls the stem of his wine glass, his dark eyes fixed on mine.

'Samos probably for a day or two, then I'll probably head to Rhodes and fly home from there.'

'And then?'

'Who knows. I hate to plan.' I shrug.

He's about to say something else, when the sound of people clapping makes us turn around. To my surprise the restaurant has filled up in the past hour, as sitting in our own little bubble I've been oblivious to people arriving at the now busy restaurant. Suddenly, the waiters appear on the terrace, now dressed in traditional Greek costume, prepared to put on a show. Some music strikes up and they begin their Greek dance as the volume is turned up on some speakers.

The crowd whoop and cheer, as one of the dancers invites a diner to join them, who is quickly followed by several more. Tucked away in the corner, I'm relieved they don't ask me to join in, as other diners are only too happy to learn the steps of the dance. There's a lot of whooping and cheering. A couple who look to be in their sixties are really going for it; the tanned wife, who has blonde hair piled into a skyscraper like Marge Simpson, is wearing gold bracelets that jangle as she dances, her bald husband beside her looking as though he's having the time of his life and I smile to myself thinking that this is what holidays are all about.

'That looks like a laugh, are you sure you don't want to dance?' I ask Georgios.

'Positive,' he says, a serious expression crossing his face, and I regret asking.

'You get up if you want,' he says a little more gently, probably regretting his moody tone.

'No, I'm fine,' I reply as the glorious feel of the evening has suddenly evaporated.

'Would you like to go for a walk?' asks Georgios. 'That is, when the waiters have stopped dancing and I can ask for the bill.' He smiles.

'Yes, okay, I'd like that. I can't be out too late though.' I glance at my watch. 'Early morning yoga on the beach tomorrow, with our host Theo.'

'Okay. Maybe just a walk along the beach a little way, as it's such a beautiful evening,' he suggests.

Shortly afterwards, Georgios settles the bill, batting away any suggestion of me at least paying my half, and realising he will not allow it, I thank him.

Walking past the stacked-up sunbeds, watching the gently rolling waves feels so relaxing. I take off my sandals and wander along the soft sand, enjoying the feel of the cool sand beneath my feet. Lights are twinkling from distant islands and Georgios stops for a minute and points into the distance.

'That's Patmos, where you will be heading to,' he tells me.

The sea, that looks so turquoise and inviting during the day, looks dark and slightly hostile in the evening, although the island looks as though it is merely a touch away. It feels like almost an echo of my feelings about my journey there, the excitement and trepidation of what I might find on that island.

Talking as we walk feels so natural and I find the darkness here thrilling, almost wishing Georgios would slip his hand into mine, but he doesn't. Eventually, we cut down a side road that leads away from the beach and back to the car park, where we climb into Georgios' car. We drive past bars with people spilling out of them, others sat outside sipping drinks beneath the moonlight, gazing into each other's eyes.

Before long we arrive back at the hotel, to the sound of laughter coming from the bar area around the pool, and Brady and Iris call us over to join them.

'Hi there, how are you guys?' asks Brady.

We take a seat and I order a brandy as a nightcap.

'Good, thanks. What have you been up to today?' I ask in return.

Brady and Iris tell us about a boat trip they have been on from Kos Harbour, called the Three Island tour.

'Oh, it was so wonderful,' says Iris. 'We pulled into a blue lagoon and had a lovely swim. As we sailed across to the island of Pserimos, we even spotted some dolphins, didn't we, Brady?' Iris sighs with pleasure.

'We sure did. It was the most wonderful sight, watching them leaping about like that.' Brady nods.

'After that, we stopped at Port Vathi and wandered around the little backstreets. I bought some souvenirs of our trip, including this.' Iris wraps her silk, colourful kimono around her, in pretty shades of the Mediterranean Sea.

'It's beautiful and your day out sounds like it was a real adventure.'

'Unforgettable,' says Iris. 'Have you guys been out together?' she asks, glancing between us both.

'We have. Georgios found a little restaurant near the beach where there was Greek dancing and the most fabulous food.' I sigh, thinking of the intimate moment we seemed to be sharing, before the Greek dancing began.

Brady asks for the name of the restaurant, and he and Georgios begin a conversation.

'Talking of food, will you be here for the BBQ Friday evening?' asks Iris as she picks at some crisps from a bowl on the table.

'Yes, it should be fun,' I say. 'Chloe and Amy are coming too so I'm looking forward to hearing what they have been up to.'

'Oh, me too. They're so full of fun, it makes me wonder how I got to be so old.' She laughs.

'You're not old. You pack so much into your days, you would put a lot of younger people to shame.' I brush off her comments.

'Well, thanks. And maybe you're right. Having a near-death experience kind of makes you live for the day,' she tells me.

'A near-death experience, really?'

Iris tells me about a time when she and Brady were out walking along a coastal path, near a cliff edge.

'Suddenly, from nowhere, a dog comes bounding along the footpath, knocking me off my feet,' says Iris. 'I fell onto a small ledge beneath and managed to hold on until Brady pulled me up. A few feet either way and I would have plunged to my death on the rocks below.'

Her hand goes to her throat and she takes a sip of her

brandy. Hearing her story, Brady reaches over and squeezes her hand.

It makes me realise just how fragile life really is, and reinforces my belief that I am doing the right thing, getting out and exploring the world and making the most of every day.

I could sit and listen to Iris's stories all evening but as I want to be up with the lark tomorrow, I finish my brandy and decide to head upstairs to bed. Georgios looks as though he is settled in for the evening, chatting to Brady and Iris, who have now been joined by Sophia.

'Well, goodnight then, and thank you for this evening, Georgios, I really enjoyed it.' I turn to him as I'm about to head upstairs.

'You're most welcome,' he says casually, resuming his conversation with Brady.

As I head off, I feel a surprising sense of disappointment that he never offered to escort me to my room, or try to kiss me, and wonder what on earth is going through his head? Or mine for that matter. This guy is proving to be someone I just can't seem to figure out.

FIFTEEN

The beach is empty apart from the yoga group assembled near the water's edge, a few of the others making their way across the sand as a gentle sea mist clears and the outline of the sun appears. I find it hauntingly beautiful at this hour.

Rose is limbering up, doing some stretches, and is in a warrior pose as I approach.

'Good morning! How are you today?' she asks, straightening up.

She looks glowing, in a blue leotard over white leggings, her shiny mahogany hair held up in a clip. Theo is scrolling through his phone and lifts his head and says '*Kalimera*' when he notices me, before coming over and handing me a mat.

'Thanks, Theo. I should buy one really, but I'm not going to be here for much longer,' I explain.

'Of course, I would not expect you to.' He smiles understandingly.

The rest of the group arrive and soon enough we are listening to Theo's instructions as he starts with some gentle stretches, before we move on to the more strenuous poses. There's no need for any background music here, as the sound of the rolling sea gently caressing the sand is enough to relax even the most stressed mind.

Despite this, I find my thoughts turning to Georgios and our wonderful evening together. Did he feel the connection that I did? I wonder. The evening at the restaurant felt so magical, yet his goodnight was perfunctory. What did I expect? He knows I'm heading off in a few days' time, which I am looking forward to, of course, but I felt like there had been a connection between us. Perhaps I was wrong and had imagined something that wasn't there. To my surprise, I find myself longing for something more, even though I'm happily single. Aren't I?

Walking across the beach an hour later, after a refreshing swim, I see Rose and Theo splashing about in the water. I smile to myself, thinking of how we should never judge other people who are taking a chance at happiness. Whether or not things develop between them, at least they are both having fun and hurting no one.

'Orla, good morning.'

I hear a voice behind me, and it's Jack dressed in black running shorts and vest, and taking a drink from his water bottle.

'Hi there, Jack. How's things?' I ask as he recovers his breath.

'Really good. Business is booming, so I can't complain.' His smile is as bright as the rising sun. 'I've just finished my morning run. Fancy a coffee?' He nods to a nearby beach bar that has just opened.

'Sure, why not,' I say, always happy to enjoy a little of Jack's company.

We sit at the white-painted wooden table that has matching chairs and a blue-checked tablecloth, with vases of fake blue flowers in the centre. The waves are lapping at the water's edge as I sip fresh orange juice and Jack drinks a coffee.

'What are your plans for the day then?' he asks as I order an omelette, deciding not to eat breakfast at the hotel this morning.

'I'm not sure really. No need to ask you what you'll be doing though, hey?'

'Actually, I have a day off,' he tells me.

'A day off, really?'

'Even us pirates are allowed the occasional day off, you know.' He laughs.

'Sorry, of course you are! Do you have a stand-in then?' I ask, sipping my freshly squeezed orange juice.

'Exactly that, yes. Mike and I alternate our days off normally, apart from the odd trip, and the workers on board have a go at the swashbuckling pirate stuff. It works for all of us,' he says, before ordering a full English breakfast.

'I think I've kind of earned this. I did a six-mile run this morning,' he says, a satisfied look on his face. 'Which was after I'd had an early morning swim, the water was freezing.'

'That's pretty impressive.'

'The freezing swim or the six-mile run?'

'Both I guess, although I think I'll stick to my yoga.'

I sip my juice, watching as the sun makes its ascent, the beach now bathed in golden sunlight. Joggers are striding determinedly along the sand; a couple are throwing a ball for a dog to retrieve as the beach bars slowly fill with people looking to eat breakfast in a perfect location.

'Anyway, back to your plans for the day,' asks Jack, when we've finished our tasty freshly made breakfasts, in the most perfect location.

'As I said, none really.' I shrug.

'In that case, do you fancy accompanying me to the Old Town?'

'You don't fancy a boat trip then?' I joke.

'Funnily enough, I don't.' He smiles. 'I'm actually going to a little art gallery that sells lovely handmade gifts too. It's my mother's birthday soon and she likes to receive a gift from Greece. I take it all women like shopping, or is that a sweeping generalisation?' He pulls a face.

'Massively. I know someone who does most of her clothes shopping online, although it's counterproductive really as she returns half of the stuff,' I tell him, thinking of a colleague at Potters who does exactly that. 'She just can't stand crowds on the high street. I quite enjoy shopping, as it happens, and love the thought of visiting an art gallery.'

'Great, I'll go home and shower, and meet you back here in half an hour then,' says Jack, draining his coffee.

'We're not walking?' I say in surprise, as the Old Town is only a ten-minute walk away.

'Normally, yes, but if I have the car we might decide to go on somewhere else. If you really have no plans for the day?'

'Oh, I see. Yes, then that's perfect. I'm happy to go wherever the day takes me.'

Just over half an hour later we are both showered and ready for the day. I'm wearing one of my floaty dresses with my bikini underneath, comfortable flip-flops and sunhat. Jack is dressed in baggy cargo shorts and a once-white T-shirt.

'How long have you got left of your holiday?' asks Jack as we walk to his car. I start going into my plans, but stop as I'm surprised to find it parked down a side-street in the large driveway of a house and Jack tells me he pays a peppercorn rent to hire the space from a resident, who is an elderly widow.

'It's a bit safer than parking it on the open road near the harbour,' he explains. 'It's been bashed once too often there by careless drivers.'

Jack's car is an old camouflage army jeep, which suits him somehow. I take a seat and we're driving along the harbour road, slowing down as we approach a roundabout, when we spot Chloe and Amy waiting at a bus stop close by. Amy raises her arm and waves when she sees me, so I wave back and Jack toots the horn.

'I wonder where they're heading; shall I go back around and pull up?' asks Jack as the traffic moves and the blue and white bus eases its way towards the bus stop, the now familiar palm trees lining the boulevard and boats in the background.

'No need, but the thought was there. I have a feeling they might be heading down to Tigaki Beach. Sounds like they had a lot of fun the last time they went.' I smile to myself as I recall the waterskiing and the bikini top incident.

Jack is easy company, and I enjoy chatting to him as we drive. Every now and then waiters at the front of local cafés wave to him as we pass, and Jack returns their wave with his dazzling smile.

'You seem to know everyone,' I remark.

'That's what I love about living here. Friendly locals and great weather, what's not to like?'

A very short while later, we park up in the Old Town, and I place my straw hat on my head as the searing heat burns down. We explore the back alleyways, most with grey and white crazy-paved floors beneath our feet. Narrow houses with blue shutters have pots of pretty flowers displayed outside their pastel-coloured front doors, and colourful flowers trailing over the white walls surrounding them.

The houses give way to warrens of shops and cafés rubbing shoulders with each other and soon enough, we are stood outside the gallery and gift shop that Jack described. Outside is a tree with bare branches in a large pot, draped with stunning necklaces made from seashells. Another stand displays leather bracelets in every colour, and I think about Georgios and how he likes to wear leather jewellery. We step inside, where I discover the most enchanting shop, with art displayed on every wall, from seascapes to paintings of the Old Town we are in, featuring houses with blue doors and ginger cats sat on doorsteps.

Jack's eyes fall on a striking silver necklace with pretty jewels; some are pearl, others in iridescent shades of mauve and silver.

'I think Mum would really like this,' he says, lifting the necklace from its stand and attracting the attention of the shopkeeper.

I notice some watercolour pencils on display in a small section selling art equipment and buy them along with a sketchpad.

Ten minutes later, after Jack has purchased the necklace and I have also bought a leather bracelet, I step outside once more into the dazzling sunshine.

'It's a hot one today,' says Jack. 'Fancy an ice cream?'

'Sure, why not?'

Jack buys us both a cornet from an ice-cream stand, vanilla for him and pistachio for me, and we take a seat on a bench beneath the shade of a tree, adjacent to a whitewashed church with a heavy wooden door.

'So, what do you do for a living?' asks Jack and I tell him about my work as a sales clerk at Potters, leaving out the fact that it's the first time I've settled anywhere. Lately, relaying my story to others has made me feel a little immature, although the longer you are single and travelling, I think it becomes more difficult to put down roots somewhere.

'How about you? Surely it wasn't your life's ambition to become a pirate?' I ask. 'Or maybe it was?'

'Not really, although watching the *Pirates of the Caribbean* movies as a kid did make it seem rather adventurous. But I was actually working as an accountant in the UK before I came here,' he tells me.

'An accountant, wow. That was the last thing I expected to

hear. Talk about an extreme career change,' I say, a little shocked.

'I know. One day, I just sat at a desk going through a client's invoices, and invariably trying to save them some money, which they constantly reminded me of, and I just I thought to myself, there's got to be more to life than this, if you see what I mean.'

'I do, actually. In fact, you and I probably have more in common than you realise,' I say, without revealing too much.

'I was single at the time, so I guess I just thought to myself, it's now or never,' he continues.

'So, no regrets?'

'None. In fact, it's the best move I made. And, of course, I'm a qualified accountant, so I could return to that life any time I want, as my mother often reminds me,' he says with a laugh.

'I agree being alone gives you the freedom to just take off and go where you want. Although I'm aware it isn't financially possible for a lot of people. I guess I'm very lucky.'

I have the security of my insurance payout in the bank, but thinking about it, I would probably have just taken off anyway and worked in bars and restaurants to make ends meet, as I've always had the wanderlust. I think if you desire something enough, there is usually no stopping you.

We amble along the narrow streets, stopping to admire things in shop windows and Jack is rather taken with a shop that sells knives and daggers of every description.

'I hope you're looking at these from a pirate's perspective?' I ask, raising an eyebrow as I follow him inside.

'I am indeed. I could never use the real thing on board the ship. All weapons are strictly plastic, health and safety and all that.'

Half an hour later, after stopping for a coffee at an outside café – where three stray kittens are weaving their way in and out of the tables, hoping for food scraps – we stroll back towards the car.

'Thanks for that, Jack, it really was an unexpected pleasure coming here today. This part of town is really wonderful.'

'You're welcome. I've enjoyed the company. I think I'm going to spend the remainder of the day chilling out on the beach before hanging out with some friends tonight. I might even head over to Mambo's later in the evening, if you're about.'

'I might do, I'm not sure what my own plans are yet.'

Dropping me off at the harbour, Jack kisses me on the cheek, and we say our goodbyes. Out of the corner of my eye, I see someone familiar emerging from a shop and looking in my direction. It's Georgios.

SIXTEEN

'Georgios, hi.' I wave over, as he walks towards me, clutching a carrier bag.

'Hi.'

'Are you taking a break from the writing? Hope it's going well.'

'Not too bad.' His gaze follows Jack, who is heading off towards his boat.

I find myself telling him about my shopping trip in the Old Town with Jack, even though he never asked.

'That's nice,' he says, not sounding as if he really means it.

'It was actually. It's so pretty, all those winding backstreets and cute gift shops. And the cats. I especially loved the little kittens.' I can hear myself babbling on as we walk, wondering why I am even explaining myself to him.

Passing Neptune's, he suddenly stops.

'Did you eat in the Old Town? If not, do you feel like joining me? That is, if I'm not stepping on anyone else's toes.'

'Jack?' I laugh. 'No, not at all. He's just a friend. I bumped into him this morning after my yoga session and he asked me if I fancied joining him on a shopping trip to look for a birthday gift for his mother.' I can hear myself rambling on once more.

Georgios regards me closely. 'Well, you looked like more than friends to me,' he says.

'I don't know what you think you saw, but it was a friendly hug. I was thanking Jack for buying me a drink. Oh, and an ice cream.'

The cheek of this guy!

I decide to take a deep breath and just say exactly what is on my mind, instead of trying to second-guess his thoughts.

'What is it to you anyway? I'm clearly nothing more than your hotel neighbour, am I?' My heart is beating so fast I'm sure he must be able to hear it.

Annoyingly, Georgios says nothing for a few seconds. When he does answer, he avoids my question completely.

'So, are you hungry?'

'What? Well, yes, a little I suppose,' I reply, disarmed by his calm demeanour.

'In that case, would you like you join me for some lunch?'

'Sure, lead the way,' I say, so we enter the restaurant, which is fairly busy with a lunchtime service.

Georgios' sister emerges from the kitchen, greeting her brother with a kiss on both cheeks. She is pretty and smiling, and today wearing her long dark hair in plaits. Georgios introduces us, and I'm surprised that she remembers me from the evening when I dined alone.

'I remember your hair,' she says. 'It's so pretty.'

I thank her, as I touch my pink-streaked hair, thinking it's probably time for a change really.

'May I recommend the catch of the day. Fresh calamari,' she tells us brightly.

'Octopus. Hmm, I'm not too sure, although, to be honest, I've never actually tried it.'

'You might be surprised. Lightly battered and drizzled with

lemon, it's actually quite delicious,' Georgios tells me. 'At least, I believe so.'

'Sold. And a Greek salad, please.' I close my menu and I agree to the white wine choice Georgios has made, of which he orders a bottle. I decide to try and enjoy my late lunch with Georgios and accept it gratefully.

'So, tell me a bit more about your latest novel,' I ask, taking a sip of the wine when it arrives, hoping to get a sneak preview of his next bestseller.

'I told you, it's a romance novel. You know my style,' he says vaguely, taking a sip of his wine.

'Is that all I'm going to get?'

'Yup.' He smiles, his gorgeous brown eyes crinkling at the corners as he does. 'I've already told you, my books kind of evolve as they go along.'

'Do you find it easier to write romance or crime thrillers?'

'There's no comparison really, as they are so different. There's a bit more artistic licence with romantic fiction though, so I like that. I have to do more research with the crime,' he reveals. 'A reader will always let you know if you have even the slightest error in the police procedure, for example. I normally find love stories quite easy to write about, but I guess I'm not really in the mood to write about finding a perfect love. I'm not even sure there is any such thing.'

'Why not?' I press.

'I found it hard to write about everlasting love after...' He pauses for a moment. 'After the person I thought was the love of my life ended things between us,' he tells me, before taking another glug of his wine.

'Oh, Georgios, I'm so sorry. I can imagine how you might have found it difficult to write a love story under the circumstances.'

In fact, I can't think of anything worse than having to write a love story when you are feeling heartbroken.

'It's silly really, because it's been more than a year since we split and I'm over it now,' he continues. 'But when I came to write the book, I just wasn't feeling it. I had to rewrite the first few chapters, which were so bad they would never have been accepted by a publisher if it was a first submission. I had to do them again, which is why I'm behind with my schedule. My editor has been on my back constantly. I think she's worried I have lost my ability to write. I do worry about that myself.' He takes another long drink of his wine.

'You think you've literally lost the plot,' I say, before wondering if I've made an ill-judged joke, but thankfully he laughs.

'Something like that. Since being here in Greece, at least things seem to be coming together. Or should I say, I have at least made some progress. I think I definitely did the right thing in coming here. Rainy London wasn't quite so inspiring.'

'Well, I'm sure it will be a huge success, just like all your other novels,' I say brightly.

'I hope you're right.'

'So, I'm not even going to get a teaser of what the book is about?'

I take a forkful of tasty Greek salad, bursting with flavour from the huge red tomatoes and crumbly feta cheese.

'Well, it's a love story so obviously it has a happy ending, even though life doesn't always go according to plan,' he says, a hint of regret in his voice. 'But, of course, I have to think of my reader. It's my job to entertain them and give them some escapism for a while.'

'And hope. When people read those novels it makes them feel that the right one is definitely out there somewhere.'

'Is that how you feel too?'

'I'm not sure,' I tell him honestly. 'I question whether or not I'm a good partner.' I find myself revealing my inner thoughts.

'Why on earth would you say that?' He looks a little taken aback.

'Oh, I don't know, I just think I'm far too restless,' I confess. 'I've never lived with anyone. I've always rented a flat, periodically heading back to my family home. My last relationship was really good, we had a lot of fun, then he started talking about settling down and getting a place together and I kind of ran away. I ended things and went to work as a nanny for a couple of months in France.'

'It sounds to me like you just haven't met the right person,' he says, echoing the words of Rose. 'Being in a partnership with someone may not necessarily stop you from feeling restless though, that's just a part of who you are.'

'I suppose it is.'

'The right partner would understand that, surely?'

'Would they?'

'I'm sure they would. But I guarantee, if you find your one true love, you probably won't want to wander too far anyway. Or maybe you would want to do things together?'

'Perhaps you're right. Gosh, relationships are so complicated, aren't they? Anyway, back to the book. So, you're definitely not giving anything away then?'

'Nope. But I will tell you that it's a slow burn of a romance, which is more realistic as far as I'm concerned. I'm not sure there is any such thing as love at first sight. Lust yes, love no,' he says with conviction. His expression changes then, so I guess that's the end of the conversation.

Our main course arrives, and I take a tentative bite of the calamari, but find it quite delicious, with its light crispy batter and drizzled with lemon juice.

'This is actually lovely, not what I expected at all,' I say as I enjoy the food.

'If its cooked correctly, it's delicious,' he agrees, biting into his own calamari. As we eat our delicious meal and with the wine I've been enjoying, I can feel myself beginning to relax.

'What are you looking at?' I say, when I find him gazing at me intensely.

'Sorry, I'm just trying to work you out, that's all. A beautiful woman, travelling all alone?'

I find myself blushing when he calls me beautiful.

'I told you my story. I want to see the world,' I say. 'I'm just grateful to be alive. And I don't think it unusual at all for a woman to be travelling alone these days, and I always meet people on my travels. And that's rich, you trying to work me out,' I say bravely, sipping my wine. 'You're a right moody Malcolm.'

'A what?' He's smiling, despite my insult.

'A moody Malcolm. Although maybe I understand why, if the novel has been a bit of a slog.'

'Sorry. Maybe I have. I could say it's in my DNA, as I'm a temperamental creative type, but it wouldn't be true. I guess I'm just plain old cranky sometimes,' he admits.

I laugh and raise my glass to that.

'Anyway, back to you. I don't see anything wrong with wanting to see the world. Just as long as you're not running away from life, because you do know it has a habit of catching up with you,' he advises, which irritates me.

'Oh, so you're a counsellor now, as well as an author, are you?' I say a little sharply.

'No, of course not. I didn't mean to offend you. I'm just saying, a lot of people run away from things, but the issues will always be there if you don't confront them.'

I wipe my mouth with a napkin and stand to leave. 'Thanks for lunch, Georgios, but I need to go back to the hotel now,' I say, trying to keep my voice even, surprised at myself for feeling so annoyed by his comments.

'Wait, I'm so sorry, please, Orla, stay for a while. I'm not sure why you're suddenly so wound up.'

'I'm not, really.' I manage to muster up a smile. 'I promised Dad I'd call him around now.' I glance at my watch. 'Thank you for lunch, Georgios, no doubt, I'll see you later.'

Walking out, I can feel the tears threatening to spill over and when I arrive at the hotel car park, I climb into my car and drive to a secluded beach I know, several miles away. There are a couple of cars in the car park, and one or two people are sat outside a refreshment van on metal chairs chatting to the owner. He greets me with a 'Kalispera' as I approach.

I buy a coffee then walk along the sand and shingle beach, which is deserted apart from a couple who are strolling along with their arms around each other. The sea is a little wild today, and I can hear the rolling waves as I walk to the water's edge. Despite my reaction to Georgios' words, I mull them over as I stare out to sea. His words echo in my ears along with the whistling of the wind. 'You can't run away from life. It has a habit of catching up with you.' I know he's right, of course, which is why this trip is all about confronting something I never thought I would have to. But it's too important to run away from.

SEVENTEEN

I hadn't realised how long I'd walked along that beach, gathering my thoughts, but it is almost seven o'clock by the time I arrive back at the hotel.

Chloe and Amy are sat near the bar as Theo shakes up a cocktail for them.

'Hey, Orla, fancy joining us?' shouts Amy as I'm about to head to my room for a shower.

'Oh, go on then,' I say, thinking maybe a cocktail is exactly what I need right now.

'We're having a mojito,' says Amy cheerfully.

'Sounds good.' I smile as I join them around the bar. 'I'll have one of those too, when you're ready, please, Theo.'

'Coming up.' He smiles.

He pours Chloe's drink into a cocktail glass, Amy already sipping hers through a black straw. The girls are looking lovely this evening, both sporting a nice tan and wearing maxi dresses and their hair curled. Amy's dress is a pretty emerald-green shade and Chloe's a multi-coloured pattern and they look ready to party the night away.

'Did you have a nice time with Jack today? You lucky thing,' Chloe says with a sigh.

'I did, actually, yes. We went shopping in the Old Town. He was going to offer you a lift somewhere, then your bus turned up,' I tell her as Theo pours the ingredients into the shaker for my mojito, and theatrically shakes it from side to side, which has us all smiling.

'Just my luck,' she says. 'So, you two are definitely not an item then?'

'Nope. Definitely not.'

I think of Jack's million-dollar smile and easy-going manner. No deep thoughts or quizzing me about my life. He's such easy company. I'd be more than happy to spend more time with him.

'Mmm, lovely. Thanks, Theo, that really is delicious,' I say after taking a sip of the refreshing, zesty cocktail, enjoying the hint of mint.

'Jack's so gorgeous. Although I imagine you could take your pick of blokes, if it's a holiday romance you're after,' says Chloe.

'So that is how you see us Greek men. Nothing more than a holiday romance.' Theo feigns a sad expression, placing his hand on his heart.

'Ha ha, I couldn't see you complaining,' Amy replies laughing and I tend to agree as I think about his dalliance with Rose, which I keep to myself.

'Anyway, what do you mean? Take my pick of men for a holiday romance?' I ask, sipping my cocktail.

'Oh, come on, you're gorgeous, you remind me of Marilyn Monroe. I've seen the way Georgios looks at you, too, and don't say you haven't noticed.'

'I haven't, actually. And who says I'm even interested in a holiday romance? Just because you've got the hots for Jack, doesn't mean I'm looking for anyone,' I say, although I can't help feeling secretly pleased that Chloe has caught Georgios looking at me.

'You have the hots for Jack?' says Theo, who is wiping the bar with a cloth. 'Jack the pirate?'

'Maybe,' says Chloe, looking slightly embarrassed. 'I think I've lost my touch though. I've been flirting with him every time I see him, but he doesn't seem to notice.'

A serious expression crosses Theo's face. 'I wouldn't bother with him,' he reveals.

'And why is that?' says Chloe, frowning.

'Let's just say that he has a bad reputation around here. He meets women who are here on holiday, then discards them like a rag, before moving on to the next one.' He pulls a face. 'Don't say I didn't warn you.'

'I can see how all the women fall for him though,' I say. 'He is a very charming man.'

Theo's jaw seems to tighten, and I wonder for a second if he might be jealous of Jack, but I can't think why.

'Well, I am just warning you, that is all. Around here, he has the reputation of a dog.'

He takes some glasses from a shelf and cleans them with a cloth until they shine.

'Well, I'm absolutely gutted. I certainly don't want to be another notch on his bedpost,' Chloe huffs, before quickly adding, 'Not that I'm saying I would sleep with him.' She takes a sip of her drink. 'Thanks for the heads-up.'

'No problem. I would hate to see a beautiful woman like you get hurt by the likes of him.' He winks, giving her a slow, sexy smile, and I wonder whether Rose is aware that he is such a flirt around other women.

'Well, thanks.' Chloe sits up and throws her long hair over her shoulder.

I'm surprised at Theo's revelation about Jack as I never saw a hint of anything flirtatious or sexual pass between Jack and me, or any inappropriate behaviour on his part. In fact, he was the perfect gentleman when I think of the evening he walked me home and never tried anything on. Perhaps it's simply that he doesn't fancy me. Poor Chloe. She's had her eye on Jack from the minute she arrived here on holiday.

'Where are you off to this evening then?' I ask Amy and Chloe as we enjoy our drinks.

'We're going to a place across the street for a pizza, then maybe we'll stroll down to Mambo's afterwards, I feel like a good dance tonight. Why don't you come with us?' they urge. I recall Jack saying he would be there this evening.

'Sure, why not? I'll maybe skip the pizza though and see you at Mambo's later on. Jack might be there, I kind of said we'd have a friendly drink later. Just letting you know.'

'It's fine.' Chloe smiles. 'He's still good company, even though I definitely don't think I'll be anything more than a mate. Oh well, never mind. Plenty more fish in the gorgeous Greek sea.' She casts a sideways glance at Theo, who is lifting a crate of beer onto a shelf, his toned arm muscles on display in his black T-shirt.

I've spotted a tiny restaurant tucked down a side street, that Sophia told me has a really good reputation for its moussaka, so I might head there for dinner later. I fancy eating alone this evening and thinking about the next part of my journey to Patmos in a couple of days' time.

'Great. How about you, Theo, do you fancy coming with us?' Amy asks him.

'I'm working here,' he reminds her. 'It is a hotel, remember. Although, if guests are not around the pool later, I may join you for a drink.' He locks eyes with Amy, giving that seductive smile once more and I can sense a frisson between them.

Talk turns to the BBQ tomorrow evening, when Sophia appears and lights candles on the long table, where guests usually assemble later in the evening, as she usually does. Lights that have come on around the pool area are reflecting on the water, casting a soft ripple effect. Sophia tells us all of the guests will be attending the BBQ, and I find myself feeling surprised that Georgios has accepted the invitation, given his pressing writing schedule and desire to be alone. She informs us that Theo is bringing a friend along and I wonder whether it might be Rose. Or maybe not, given his flirtatious behaviour with Amy this evening.

'I've invited someone too,' she says, looking a little coy. 'It's someone from my bank, which I hope isn't inappropriate.'

'I don't see why,' I venture. 'We can meet friends in the most unexpected situations, can't we?' I say, recalling how I once met a bloke who sat next to me in the accident and emergency department of the local hospital. He was a builder, who'd cut his hand with an electric saw. I'd burnt my hand on the oven. We dated for around three months.

'Yes! You are right. Most unexpected, indeed. I have no interest in men since my husband died, but something passed between us.'

'What's his name?' I ask with interest.

'It's Yiannis and he will be retiring next year. He sadly lost his wife three years ago. He told me all about it over coffee when we were discussing the terms of the loan for the extension,' she tells us. 'Oh, and I must add, he is most handsome.'

Theo is rolling his eyes in the background, muttering something about his mother acting like a lovesick teenager.

'Well, I for one am looking forward to the BBQ. I'm going to drive down to Kefalos tomorrow and spend the day there, so it will be nice to relax here for the evening when I get back,' I say. 'And I'm looking forward to meeting your friend.'

'Thank you, Orla. Kefalos has a nice beach. Are you going to swim across to the islet with the little church?' Sophia asks as she finishes lighting the candles that have cast a soft glow in the seating area.

'I'm actually thinking about it,' I tell her. 'I've been to Kefalos before and spent some time on the beach there. I'm not sure whether I might need a pedalo though, as it's been a while since I've swum any distance.'

'It isn't far at all,' she reassures me. 'Or if you swim at the beach, I would at least take a snorkel and some swimming goggles,' she advises. 'The sea is very clear there and you might even see some pretty fish.'

'I might just do that, it sounds lovely.'

The little island, which is called Kastri, is opposite the beach at Aghios Stefanos near Kefalos, and from what I remember attracts lots of visitors, many of whom swim across to it from the beach. There isn't much to see apart from the white church with a blue roof, as the rest of the island is rocky and barren. There is nothing else there, apart from the rocky remains of an old fort at the top of a hill that used to guard the bay from enemies and pirates in days gone by. It's said the little church is dedicated to St Nicholas, thought to be the protector of sailors.

I finish my delicious cocktail, then head upstairs to ring Dad before I take a shower.

Dad's phone rings out, so I leave him a voicemail and ten minutes later as I'm about to step into the shower, he returns my call, telling me he is watching the snooker.

'Sorry, love, I was just making a cuppa, while there's a break.'

'There usually is in a game of snooker,' I joke.

'Oh, ha ha. I mean an interval. My phone was in the other room, I never heard it ring.'

'Don't worry, and I won't keep you long if you're watching the snooker. How are you?' I ask.

'I'm fine, thanks, love. I've been out on a walk today, with Betty from across the road,' he tells me.

A picture pops into my mind of Mum and Betty having a cuppa together in our dining room, Betty often bringing one of her delicious Victoria sponges over.

'A walk? That sounds nice. Where did you go?' I'm so happy Dad is keeping himself busy.

'We had a canal walk in a village not far from Wigan. I took the car out for a little run.' I can hear the sound of him stirring his tea with a spoon.

Betty's husband Phil passed away suddenly last year and I know from chatting to her from time to time that she misses him terribly.

'That sounds lovely, Dad. Fresh air and exercise will do you both good. How is Betty?'

'Oh, you know, not too bad. She misses Phil a lot though. I thought a little walk in the fresh air might do her good, put some colour in her cheeks. We had a spot of lunch at a lovely old pub called The Ship.'

'That's really kind, Dad, you're a good neighbour and friend,' I say, feeling proud of him, yet once more feeling at odds with his behaviour all those years ago...

'Thanks, love. I think it really brightened her up, as she was smiling a lot when we got home. I haven't seen her smile like that in a while. I suggested the same time next week, although I think we'll go somewhere different. I've got a book somewhere of Cheshire walks that I might dig out.'

'As long as it's not in the attic. I don't want you climbing ladders when I'm not there,' I warn him and he promises me that he won't.

'And you can probably download walks from Google onto your phone,' I advise him.

I feel thrilled that Dad is getting on with his life and I can't think of a nicer person than Betty for him to spend some time with. Dad asks me how the holiday is going and I tell him I'm having a lovely time and fill him in on the places I've been visiting. I try to remain as upbeat as possible, thinking of the lovely father he has been to me and not let recent revelations destroy those memories.

'Make sure you take lots of photos,' he says, before telling me that the next frame of the snooker is about to start, so we wrap up the call.

As I stand beneath the hot shower, I think about my lunch with Georgios earlier and wonder why I reacted the way I did. Maybe he touched a nerve when he said we can't run away from our problems. Because the fact is, he is right. If there is some unresolved issue in your life it will always be there, gnawing away at you. Even if you travel to the ends of the earth.

EIGHTEEN

I choose a long, black cheesecloth dress and backcomb my hair slightly to give it a tousled look, before applying Strawberry Fool lipstick and a spray of my evening perfume.

The evening is warm and balmy, the sky streaked with shades of orange and violet when I head out, just after eight thirty. It's busy along the harbour front, but as soon as I step down the side street, away from the main drag, the sound of laughter and chatter from outside bars is replaced with the sound of traditional Greek music. The Seashell taverna is extremely busy, and I wonder whether I ought to have made a reservation. I'm considering walking past when a waiter wishes me a good evening, before showing me to a table set for two.

'I hope this is okay?' he says politely and I tell him, yes, it's perfect. The table is tucked into a little alcove with a window that gives a side view of the sea. I order a drink, and he returns with a menu.

'I've heard the moussaka is a must-have here, so I'll have that, please.'

'Thank you. I am sure you will not be disappointed,' he says, before disappearing into the kitchen with my order.

I glance around the cosy restaurant that has dark-panelled walls and wooden tables covered in red tablecloths, with chunky cream pillar candles at the centre, giving it a relaxed, almost homely feel. The dark walls are adorned with foodie pictures, such as lemons and peppers and traditional Greek dishes. It looks authentic, and simple, and I'm hoping the food will be a real taste of Greece.

Glancing around, I notice that there is a mixture of Greek diners, as well as holidaymakers, which I think is always a good endorsement of a restaurant. A large family are sat at a long table clearly celebrating, as a waitress appears carrying a cake adorned with lit sparklers and everyone breaks into applause. The whole of the restaurant joins in when the waiters sing 'Happy Birthday', and I sing along too, soaking up the wonderful atmosphere.

Sitting here enjoying a perfectly lovely evening, a memory flashes into my mind. I'm pretty sure I have been to this restaurant when I was a child, as glancing out of the window there is a little park with a see-saw and a slide. It tugs at my heartstrings when I think of Mum and Dad sitting on the other end of the see-saw, me being flung as high as the sky, at least in my young eyes. I used to long to have a sibling with me, so that Mum and Dad could have sat inside the restaurant waiting for us, like other parents did, sipping a drink, instead of having to be my playmate. I think about the sister I never knew I had, but push the thought firmly away as my delicious-looking moussaka arrives, served in a terracotta pot, the aroma making my stomach rumble as it reaches my nostrils.

'*Efcharisto*,' I say, as the waiter places the food in front of me. I take a sip of my wine and dive right in, devouring the tasty meat and aubergine dish, rich with béchamel sauce that has just the right amount of cinnamon. Gosh, Sophia was right to recommend this place. The moussaka is the best I have tried in a long while.

Resisting a dessert, I am presented with some fresh melon slices at the end of the meal and a shot of ouzo.

'I remember coming here as a child,' I find myself telling the waiter as he clears away my plates. 'Is it the same family that own the restaurant?' I ask, unable to recall the name of it back then.

'Yes, it is. Francine and Stavros, who still cook in the kitchen now, they are my parents.' He smiles.

A few minutes later, a lady in her sixties comes out to speak to me, when I offer my compliments to the chef.

'I am happy you enjoy the moussaka, *efcharisto*. My son tells me you come here as a child?' she asks; her English is quite good, although not fluent.

'I was around ten years old, I think,' I tell her. 'I actually remember the little park outside.'

'My son used to play on the park also. Maybe you sit side by side on the swing, he is maybe your age.' She speaks her words slowly, making sure her English is correct. 'I am happy you return to Kos. Maybe you don't leave it so long next time,' she says, before returning to the kitchen.

'Maybe I won't.'

A few minutes later, her smiling husband appears and offers me another shot of ouzo, which I decline, as it's pretty strong stuff.

'I hope you come and see us again,' says her husband. 'Enjoy the rest of your holiday.'

'Actually, may I get a photo? I will show it to my father when I get home.'

'But, of course!'

He calls out in Greek, beckoning his wife and son to join us too, and I think it's a shame the older one isn't about, as we could have swapped stories of playing in the park outside. Maybe he would have remembered me and we could have walked off into the sunset together and lived happily ever after. I can't help thinking that would make a good storyline for a book, so maybe I'll suggest it to Georgios.

Stavros asks another waiter if she would mind taking a photo of me with the family that I will show to my father when I get home, so we smile for the camera as the waitress takes the shot.

'Lovely, thank you so much,' I say, after viewing the photo on my phone and I glance at the smiling faces in the picture.

The thought of family preoccupies my thoughts as I head off a little after nine thirty, despite me trying to push it to the back of my mind. It would have been nice to have a sister, and I can't help wondering if it's too late to begin a relationship with a sibling you only found out about in later life, like you see on those family reunion shows.

The sky has darkened a little and as I walk the stars begin to appear in a grey sky. The noise and lights from the bars guide my path as I make my way towards Mambo's; the music puts me straight back into holiday mood. I'm about to enter, when I spot Amy and Chloe heading towards the bar from a different direction.

'Hi, did you enjoy your pizza?' I ask them.

'Oh, the best I've had. There's something about those wood-fired pizza ovens. I might get one when I go home,' says Amy, full of enthusiasm.

'For a two-foot balcony in a flat?' Chloe asks, laughing.

'Maybe not, although it's a bit bigger than that, and it's not a flat, it's an apartment,' she replies with a grin, referring to the three-bedroomed student accommodation she is currently sharing.

We all opt for a cocktail and take it outside, into the warm evening air and find a seat at one of the wooden tables. The noise from the sea can be heard once more, the sound of waves gradually becoming louder as the night draws in. I prefer to sit outside, as I love the sound of the crashing waves, competing with the gentle thud of the music that can be heard from inside the bar. There's something about the contrast of the two sounds that I truly love.

'I just love Kos, don't you?' says Chloe, watching the sun disappear in a rapidly darkening sky. 'I really don't want to go home.'

We're sipping mojitos, having enjoyed the one at the hotel earlier, although if I had to choose, I'd say Theo's just has the edge. Maybe it was the way he shook it.

'It's always hard going home after a great holiday,' Amy says with a deep sigh. 'I'll definitely came back here though.'

'I'm not sure I will. I mean, it's brilliant and everything, but if I have the chance to travel, I want to see different places. There's a big world out there waiting to be explored,' says Chloe, her voice full of hope for the future.

'That's true enough, but there's no harm in returning to a favourite place,' argues Amy.

'No harm at all, but how will you know if it's your favourite place if you don't have that many places to compare it to?' Chloe replies. 'I thought Disney World was my best ever holiday as a kid, then we went to the South of France when I was fifteen, and I loved it even more,' she says, with a slightly faraway look in her eyes.

'Isn't that because you had a thing for the lifeguard at the pool?' Amy raises an eyebrow. 'I remember you telling me all about that, when we were talking about our first crush.'

'I did, although it was quite innocent. I was only sixteen, he had just turned eighteen. We kissed on the last night of the holiday. It was the most wonderful kiss too.' She sighs. 'And that's my point about seeing different places and having new experiences. Phillipe was almost as thrilling as the rides in Disney

World, but in a totally different way,' she says, smiling at the memory.

'I take your point,' says Amy. 'But some people like familiarity, and enjoy things tried and tested, don't they? We're not all like you, eh, Orla?'

'I suppose I've always been a bit restless, and I do like to visit different places, so agree with Chloe, but at the same time I was keen to revisit Kos. It's where I have the best childhood memories of spending time with Mum and Dad,' I explain. 'It's a kind of comfort, especially as my mum is no longer with us.'

'Ah, I'm sorry about your mum. But it's nice that you have such lovely memories,' says Amy.

'It really is,' says Chloe, before she glances around the bar.

'You're not looking for Jack, are you?' I tease.

'What's the point?' She takes a sip of her drink.

'Oh, I don't know,' says Amy. 'Maybe he'd be a one-woman man if he fell for you. He might change his ways.'

Chloe tosses her long hair over her shoulder.

'Fall for me. Who says I want that? I'm on holiday, I was just thinking of having a bit of fun,' she says honestly. 'I'll be going home soon. But I'm not interested in someone who has such a bad reputation. I might catch something.'

'Chloe!' I say, almost spitting my drink out.

'What? It might be true. Theo has definitely put me off when he told me Jack was a serial womaniser. There's no way I'm going to be another conquest. In fact, maybe holiday romances aren't really my thing at all.' She shrugs.

'People like Jack are always going to meet lots of women, given his job and living in a place like this. Especially during the summer season,' says Amy.

'I know. Anyway. It's probably better if I stay single. I want to really concentrate on my studies this year. I've had my fill of rubbish jobs; I want to make something of myself,' she says determinedly.

'Well, good for you, Chloe.' I raise my glass. 'Let's have a toast to success.'

'To success,' the girls echo.

'Whose and what success?' Jack appears at the table with his beaming smile and sexy blonde hair, dressed in a black vest and stone-coloured shorts.

Chloe seems so happy to see him, I feel she is going to forget everything she just said about being another conquest and set about flirting with him, but she doesn't. 'Oh, you know, just life, opportunities. Second stab at a career, that sort of thing.'

As Jack orders a drink, she tells him all about her desire to become a professional photographer.

'I think it's great that you're going after what you want in life,' he tells her genuinely. 'I don't think I'll be a pirate forever. I'd actually love to retrain for something one day. I can't be a pirate for the rest of my life.'

'Why not?' asks Amy.

'Because I don't want to be an old man out on the water, shivering me timbers.' He laughs.

'But you are a trained accountant,' I remind him.

'Are you?' Amy and Chloe look equally shocked.

'Yes, but I left that profession, didn't I? So, it obviously never set me on fire. What I'd really like to do is train as an airline pilot. The courses are expensive though, so I'll have to make a few more people walk the plank first,' he muses. 'And what about you, Amy, as we're talking about careers?'

'I'm not too sure yet. I'm doing a history degree at university.'

'Interesting.' Jack nods.

'Well, I think so. I actually wouldn't mind a job in a museum; there are a few fabulous ones in Liverpool. Failing that, I wouldn't mind being a history teacher.'

'Actually, talking about my career in photography, let's get a picture of us all now,' says Chloe. She beckons a waiter over, and, after showing him how to use the camera, we group together and flash our brightest smiles. I can't help thinking it's a shame Georgios isn't here too.

'And now your turn, Orla, as you don't seem to have figured out what you want out of life yet either,' Jack says, and even though he means it good-naturedly, I can't help feeling a little embarrassed, as at the age of thirty-two, maybe it's about time I did.

'I've been thinking about it a lot since I've been here. Maybe travelling around will help me get my head together. At least I can only hope so.'

'People figure themselves out in the end, don't they?' he says positively. 'Although I think we live in a society that's so fixated on buying a house and settling down, that some people forget what they really want from their life.'

'That's true enough. So many people just do what is expected of them. If a woman decides not to have children, she's even judged for that, although it's nobody else's business. It's about time people stopped judging others, and let them live how they want to. Gosh, what are we like, putting the world to rights, hey?' I laugh.

'I propose a toast,' says Jack, raising a glass. 'Here's to finding out what we really want from life. Whatever that may be.'

'Whatever that may be,' we all chorus and raise our glasses.

Just then, a catchy dance tune strikes up from the disco, and Amy grabs me by the hand.

'Right, that's enough of the serious stuff. We have to dance to this one,' she says, pulling me towards the dance floor inside and I happily follow.

'I'll keep your seat warm,' says Jack as he stays behind chatting to Chloe, and I can't help wondering if there is a mutual attraction between them, despite what Theo has told us about him.

Inside, the dance floor is a little empty, as most people are sitting on bar stools sipping drinks from a variety of drinking vessels, including coconuts, jam jars and tall, thin glasses, not a pint pot or a wine glass to be seen. The mirrored backdrop of the bar displays every drink you can think of and the ceiling is covered in football shirts of all nations, with a ceiling fan at the centre. It's so different to all the other bars here, and almost makes me feel I might be on holiday on a Caribbean island.

As we begin to dance to the particularly catchy dance tune, the people at the bar slide off their bar stools and join us. Just then, a large group of women enter the bar and immediately dance their way to the floor, whooping and clapping and within a few minutes the place is bouncing. Continuing with the nineties theme, a Spice Girls song is played and Jack and Chloe appear from outside.

'It sounded like we were missing the party out there,' says Chloe, quickly getting into her dance moves with Jack, who's a very good mover. Chloe is pointing at him and singing the line that says something about wanting to be his lover, and I can't help wondering where this is going. A succession of catchy tunes are played, and a while later after a few more dances, I head outside for some fresh air and spot someone having a drink alone at an outside table.

'I never had this place down as being your thing,' I say to Georgios as I approach his table.

'I might say exactly the same to you,' he replies. 'I thought you liked places with a more relaxed vibe.' He swirls his beer around in his glass. He's dressed in a light blue T-shirt and dark shorts, another leather necklace around his neck.

'Usually, yes,' I admit. 'But on holiday, I just go with the flow. It's good to let your hair down now and again. Dare I ask how the book is going?'

'Actually, it's going surprisingly well. Having said that, I'm still not sure about the relationship between the main character and the love interest. It's still a little unpredictable. In fact, it's all over the place.'

'I guess that's what readers like in a story. Nothing too predictable.'

'Anyway, as I've been working for most of the day, I decided to come out for a drink. I heard you say you might be here when I was working earlier.'

'You overheard our conversation?' I mentally replay the conversation, hoping I wasn't talking about him.

'Only when you were chatting to the girls at the bar. I was working on the balcony; it isn't difficult to hear conversations below. I wasn't intentionally eavesdropping,' he explains. 'Just like you weren't when I was chatting to my editor at the restaurant.' He raises an eyebrow. 'Anyway. I was hoping to speak to you. I wanted to apologise for somehow upsetting you this afternoon,' he says sincerely, fixing me with his dark-brown eyes, that are the kind of eyes that would have me forgive him anything.

'It's not you who should be apologising. Maybe I was being a little oversensitive,' I admit.

'So, are we okay?'

I look at him, his presence so captivating sitting here beside me, the sound of the sea in the background, and I find it makes me feel happy that he's turned up here this evening. A couple of women in short dresses give him the once-over as they walk past, and I'm not surprised he is attracting attention, he really does stand out from the crowd.

'Yes, of course, we're okay. And don't worry, I won't ask you anything else about the book.'

'That's good to hear. Anyway, as I've worked nonstop all day, tonight I am taking a break so no more talk of work,' he says, but with a smile.

I want to explain to him how much his comment about running away jarred with me a little, but as I don't want to reveal my inner turmoil and ruin the light-hearted mood of the evening, I decide to say nothing.

'That's fine with me.' I paint on my brightest smile.

'Now, can I get you a drink?' Georgios offers and I accept, so we head inside together. Chloe and Amy shout over to us, beckoning me onto the dance floor and Georgios smiles as we head to the busy bar.

'So, you don't want to dance?' I ask as the whole dance floor sings along to 'Mysterious Girl'.

'I think I'll just sit this one out,' says Georgios and I agree.

The outside area is quiet, as everyone is inside in full party mode, the disco appealing to everyone in town, judging by the number of people crammed inside. Sitting at the table, sipping our drinks, Georgios asks me about my plans for the rest of the holiday.

'You mentioned going to Patmos. What day will you be leaving?' he asks.

'The day after tomorrow. I'm going to go to Kefalos tomorrow and visit the little island opposite the beach at Aghios Stefanos. I might even swim across. I was looking at the distance today, and it doesn't actually seem very far,' I tell him.

'I don't suppose it is, if you swim regularly. Do you?' he asks.

'Not lately. In truth, I've been a little worried about vigorous exercise since... well, since I've been ill. The doctor did say I can exercise now though, so swimming should be fine.'

'I'm sure it will be. It's good to get the heart pumping through physical activity.' He locks eyes with me, and I find myself averting my gaze, suddenly feeling a little flustered.

'How long will you be staying on Patmos?' he asks, thankfully returning to my travelling schedule.

'A few days, I think. I'm interested to see the cave of the

Apocalypse.' I don't tell him the real reason I've decided to head over there.

Thinking about the faith the pilgrims who flock there have, my thoughts flit to my father, and I wonder whether my mother always had faith in him, before things briefly went awry between them.

Just then, Chloe appears outside followed by Amy.

'Oh, hi, Georgios, do you fancy a dance?' asks Chloe and I'm sure he looks mildly horrified.

'Thanks, but I don't really dance,' he says. 'Two left feet.'

'Come on, you're on holiday! No one cares if you can't dance,' she persists.

'Maybe I should have said, I don't like dancing. It's not my thing. Unless it's a slow number, of course.' He glances my way and I feel my face flush. 'Besides, I think I may actually be dangerous on the dance floor.'

'Dangerous?' I ask, puzzled. 'What on earth do you mean?'

'Last time I danced was at a wedding where I stepped on my partner's feet and it set off a chain reaction.' He shakes his head and sighs.

'And?' says Amy, her eyes wide. 'What happened?'

'She lost her footing and crashed into a woman behind her, who was carrying a tray of drinks, that she spilled.' He pauses for dramatic effect. 'Then, a bloke right behind her slipped on the drink and put his back out.'

'Oh my goodness, I can picture the scene.' Amy howls, unable to contain her laughter.

'That wasn't the end of it.' He grimaces. 'As he went down, he grabbed at a young woman's dress in an effort to save himself, which turned out to be a skirt, that he pulled to her knees, revealing her lacy black underwear.'

'You are kidding!' I'm open-mouthed with shock, whilst Amy and Chloe are hysterical.

'It was a disaster. Oh, and the guy who put his back out was the father of the bride. He was less than impressed at having to sit the rest of the evening out.'

'On second thoughts, you stay away from that dance floor,' says Amy, when she has finally finished laughing. 'How about you, Orla?'

'Maybe in a little while. I'm quite enjoying the fresh air out here.'

As well as the company, I realise.

The conversation flows easily between us, and when we head inside for a drink fifteen minutes later, a slow song is being played, and couples are entwined in each other's arms, swaying along to the music. I wonder whether Georgios might ask me to dance, surprised that I feel excited at the very thought of dancing up close with him, when suddenly the DJ speaks.

'Okay, that was for all you loved-up couples who are in this evening, but the night is still young,' says the DJ. 'So let's get back to those dance tunes.' And another clubland classic shakes the dance floor.

'Fancy a dance?' I tease, shouting over the music to Georgios and he can't get out of the bar quick enough.

Just after midnight, I'm ready to head back to the hotel and Georgios says he is ready to call it a night too, so we head inside and wave to Chloe and Amy, who are still going for it on the dance floor with their seemingly endless energy. They wave wildly and blow kisses before resuming their dancing.

'Have you enjoyed tonight?' Georgios asks as we walk along the harbour front, a rainbow of lights from the many bars reflecting on the water.

'I really have. It's so different to the places I would usually visit, but I always have a lot of fun at Mambo's. I think it's good to change things up from time to time.'

'Maybe. Although there is nothing wrong with sticking to what you find comfortable,' he reasons.

'Like not being forced into dancing?'

'Exactly. It just makes me feel uncomfortable. I know I'm a terrible dancer, so why bend to the pressure?'

'I don't think we should be pressurised into anything, for sure, but I think it's good to move out of your comfort zone occasionally,' I tell him and he actually rolls his eyes.

'I like being comfortable. Why on earth is everyone so obsessed with getting out of a comfort zone?' he says. 'Surely a place of comfort should be something you strive for?'

For some reason, I find his logic annoying, despite seeing his point. I'm about to say something, but he hasn't finished yet.

'I personally think people who are constantly seeking new things and trying to break out of their so-called comfort zone are not really content with their life.'

'Oh, so you're a psychologist as well as an author, are you?' I huff; the mood of the evening has evaporated, on my part at least.

'What?' He stops walking and turns to face me, his handsome face illuminated by a street lamp. 'I'm not counselling anyone; why are you taking this so personally?' He looks a little confused. 'I'm just saying there is a lot to be said for being content and comfortable. What's wrong with sticking to the things you enjoy?'

'There's nothing wrong with that, but it's good to try out new things, is all I'm saying. Push your boundaries.'

'I understand some people might like doing that, but you should never be forced into doing something you don't find enjoyable. You know, I had a friend whose partner kept insisting they went skiing together to try something new, but he wasn't keen at all. Tony was a bit lacking in coordination, you might say, the kind of guy who could trip over a feather on the floor. Anyway, two days into the skiing trip, he took a bad fall and broke both arms. I don't think his girlfriend planned on wiping his backside until his arms were out of plaster. They split up within the year, after three years together.'

'Well, that's an extreme example, if ever I've heard one.' It's my turn to roll my eyes. 'It doesn't mean you shouldn't try different things; there's a big world out there, and life should be lived to the full.'

'That's right. Life is for living, exactly how you choose to live it, that's all I'm saying. Not dictated to by other people, or what some self-help book tells you that you ought to be doing.'

'So, you don't think it's good to try out new things?'

'I'm not saying that at all. I've tried most things in life.' He turns to look at me. 'But I'm almost forty years old, so I know what I like by now.' His intense gaze stirs something in me, despite our difference of opinion.

'I suppose you do know what you like when you get older. I just don't want to look back in later life, wishing I'd tried things, and being too old to do it. I don't want any regrets.'

'You will never regret your life if you do the things that please you. Although I guess being someone who likes to flit from place to place, I can see how you maybe can't relate to settling down and feeling content. Maybe you never give things a chance.'

'I beg your pardon?' We are stood outside the hotel now.

'I'm not being rude, just honest. Maybe, as you said earlier, you are a little oversensitive.' He's smiling but I'm angry, thankful that it's dark and he can't see the colour in my cheeks.

'Well, goodnight, Georgios.' I feign a yawn. 'See you tomorrow, no doubt. Thanks for the drinks this evening.' I try and muster up a smile.

'You're welcome. See you tomorrow,' he says, unaware of how his comments have rattled me. I'm already halfway up the stairs to my room, so barely hear his response.

Once inside my room, I remove my make-up and change into a shorts pyjama set. I pour myself a glass of water and mull over his words. I realise I'm angry because I know his words ring true and wonder why I am always running off looking for something new and, basically, running away from my life. I'm not saying we shouldn't have fun and enjoy life, but it can't be all travelling the world and having fun. Not unless you are a multi-millionaire, I guess. Maybe it's time I stopped running away from reality and accept that life has boring bits too.

NINETEEN

I wake early, and once again I hear the sound of Georgios furiously tapping away at his computer from the balcony, so I head downstairs for breakfast, somehow not feeling the need to say good morning to Georgios, which I know is childish of me. Why did I take his comments so personally? He was merely giving his point of view and we should have just debated our opinions in a grown-up manner, agreeing to disagree.

'Good morning.' Sophia is replenishing a breadbasket, and filling a jug with fresh orange juice when I approach the table.

'*Kalimera.*' I take a seat where the rest of the guests, apart from Georgios, are seated.

'How are you enjoying your holiday?' I ask Brady and Iris, who haven't been around much in the evening.

'Oh, it's wonderful, thanks. We've been exploring every inch of this island, so it's been early to bed and early to rise these past couple of days,' Brady says, explaining their absence in the late evening. 'I'm looking forward to a good old steak on the BBQ tonight though. Are you guys coming?' he asks us all and we tell him, yes, we are.

'What are your plans today, Orla?' asks Iris as she tucks into some smashed avocado and poached eggs on toast.

'I'm heading to Aghios Stefanos Beach,' I tell her. 'I thought I might swim across to the little island with the church across the water.'

'That sounds good. We looked at that from the beach, didn't we?' Brady turns to Iris. 'It sure looks pretty, although I think I'd have to take a boat over these days. I don't think I could make that swim.' He smiles, piling his plate with toast, cheese and ham. 'I think we're just going to take it easy today,' he continues. 'We're a little tired with all that sightseeing. Maybe a beach day is in order with a cocktail or two.'

'Sounds good to me,' says Amy. 'In fact, we're heading down to Lambi Beach later. There's a bar there that has a DJ during the day apparently, so that might be fun. I've heard the beach is lovely too, so might see you there.'

'Sounds good for you young people.' Brady smiles. 'But I think we might just stay around the pool, or stroll over the road to the local beach, what do you think, Iris?' he asks his wife, who nods.

'Sure. I could do with a whole day topping up my tan before we head off home. And maybe actually read one of the books I brought with me. I'll be sad to leave this place.' She sighs, but Brady reassures her they will be back to Greece the following year.

'Maybe even later in the year when it's cooler. I'd love to see the Minoan Palace of Knossos in Crete,' he says.

I've learnt from our conversations that Brady and Iris are retired, and once ran a bed and breakfast, which they loved doing until it became too much for them. It's wonderful that they are having such fun in their retirement.

After breakfast, I head upstairs for my bag and sunhat and just as I'm leaving Georgios appears at his front door.

'Good morning.' He smiles.

'Hi, good morning,' I say, before heading for the stairs.

'I hope you enjoy your day in Kefalos.'

'I hope you enjoy yours too. Are you at the BBQ this evening?' I ask, smiling and trying not to be offended by this man, who has done nothing wrong, yet his comments seem to constantly get under my skin.

'Yes, I am actually. I plan to spend the whole day writing, so I'm really looking forward to it,' he says brightly.

'Me, too. Well, I hope you have a productive day, see you later then.' I smile as I disappear into the bright sunshine. I head towards my car with my beach bag, looking forward to my day in Kefalos.

TWENTY

Before heading to the beach at Kefalos. I take a detour and make my way towards Alikes Salt Lake near Tigaki, for a nice long walk after breakfast. I park up at what looks like an almost deserted landscape with scorched grasses and shells of grey stone buildings adorned with graffiti. Walking on, I see the first glimpse of the salt lake, stretching out ahead of me beneath the bluest of skies. It's very quiet here and a world away from the busy, touristy streets. I imagine it's a place where you could absorb the solitude and really clear your head.

I'm soon on a defined path that leads towards the lake, where a flock of white birds glide across the blue and slightly pink-tinted lake. Mountains rise in the background, and the silence is so profound as there isn't currently another person in sight.

Walking on, I pass another grey building, and a bird flies out from a nest inside, startling me slightly. A little further down, I take a seat on an old wooden bench and glance across the pretty lake. Behind me are patches of white that look like snow, but must be the residue of salt from the lake. A few darker-coloured birds swoop by making a squawking sound, breaking the silence of the surroundings. Far across the lake, I spot a heron that circles before swooping down into the water for a fish. Part of the land is dry, cracked and white, making it look almost like a lunar landscape, surrounded by a blue lake and lush green forest.

Sitting here, all alone, my thoughts turn to my future. Much as I hate to admit it, Georgios suggesting I was a person who wasn't content and maybe ran away from things, resonated with me a little. Maybe I've always avoided uncomfortable situations, rather than confronting them. Every break-up, fall out with a friend, or period of grief has me moving on to pastures new, rather than resolving things. One of my early friends stole some money from me – on my first caravan holiday – and I just cut contact with her, although we all drifted off to do different things anyway after leaving school. Looking back, I think I was just so hurt by her actions, as I'd always shared everything with her, knowing she came from a family that never had much money. She did try to apologise and I hated myself for not immediately accepting her apology. I beat myself up for a while, not wanting to be this awful, unforgiving person, so a year later I contacted her and we resumed our friendship, but it was never the same. After that, I was determined I would face things in my life head-on and live with the consequences, yet somehow I struggle do it. I know that I avoid uncomfortable situations and I wish I didn't. There's something I am absolutely determined to address whilst I'm here though. Even though Dad clearly never acted upon the information he received, I am determined to do so.

A young couple with a dog stroll past saying, '*Kalimera*,' breaking me from my thoughts.

'*Kalimera*,' I reply. And the friendly, auburn-coloured dog approaches me, so I stroke it and it wags its tail madly.

When the couple move on, an elderly Greek lady takes a seat on the bench beside me. She's carrying a basket, and I wonder whether she may have been foraging in the nearby forest, as there looks to be a variety of berries and fruits in the basket. She takes a fig from the basket and offers me one.

'Efcharisto. Have you collected these things locally?' I ask, to which she replies, 'Nai,' which means yes.

'Well, thank you. Maybe I will eat it later,' I say. 'I'm still a little full after breakfast.' I slip the ripe fig into my bag and stare out across the vast lake.

'Okay?' asks the lady, who is dressed in a long, patterned dress, a black scarf tied around her head.

'What? Oh, yes, I'm okay, thanks for asking. Life can be so complicated sometimes, can't it?' I sigh.

'Nai.' She nods slowly.

'I mean, I'm here to enjoy a holiday, grateful to be alive, well aware that others are not so lucky. I just want to travel, meet new people and inhale the fresh air in new places before I move on. I don't see anything wrong in that, do you?'

She looks at me and smiles.

'But now, I've gone and met this man, that I feel so drawn to,' I confide in her. 'The problem is, he's so awkward. He thinks he knows me, making comments about me not being content, and maybe running away from life. He knows nothing of what I have been through. He even makes judgements about people who are adventurous, saying they ought to be more content, which is complete rubbish.' I can hear myself prattling away at a hundred miles an hour. 'It doesn't help that he's so bloody attractive.'

She nods slowly once more.

'Annoyingly, I even find myself wondering what he's up to when he's not around the hotel. Oh, and did I mention that he's an author. He writes romantic fiction. Ha! He must definitely delve deep into his imagination to come up with those tender love stories.'

I turn to the old lady, who is still smiling at me.

'You don't understand English, do you?' I ask.

'*Nai*.'

'Have you understood a single word I've said?'

'*Nai*.'

'I'm sorry. I hope I haven't bored you,' I apologise, smiling.

'*Nai*.'

'Well, *efcharisto*.' I hold up the fig and she smiles warmly, saying '*Parakalo*', which I know means you are welcome, before she departs. As she disappears amongst the trees, I can't help laughing to myself. And there was I thinking she was a really good listener, when she didn't understand a single thing I said.

A short while later, I continue my walk, enjoying the wild, natural landscape, and feeling surprisingly good after venting to the Greek lady. I pass one or two old, gnarled olive trees, but the land consists mainly of tall grasses and bushes in shades of deep red and green. Eventually, the path leads to the lake, where hundreds of white birds are wading in the water. A large flock suddenly take to the air, the sound of their wings flapping breaking the silence. A minute later, there's the drone of a moped approaching, and I suddenly feel a little vulnerable walking in such an isolated place. I glance around for the old woman, but she is nowhere to be seen. Turning away from the lake, I follow a path, and find a family ambling towards me, just as the moped driver rides past. I'm surprised to see that it's the old woman, her basket of foraged goods dangling from the handlebars.

Walking on, I'm delighted to spot several flamingos standing on the salt flats in a group close to the water, and take some photos with my phone. I bet Chloe would get some wonderful shots here with her fancy camera.

The lake is so vast that I decide to turn around, following the family, and make my way towards the start of the circular walk. Once more, I find myself thinking of Georgios as I walk and how surprised I was when I discovered he was a writer. I can't help finding him intriguing but it's obvious he is completely absorbed in his work and definitely not looking for a girlfriend. Maybe he is still getting over his break-up and, as he said, he struggled with the earlier chapters, finding it difficult to write about everlasting love.

It isn't long before I'm on the main road of Kefalos Harbour, the atmosphere from the lake walk completely different here as the road is busy with cars and holidaymakers walking along the beach road.

I park and walk alongside the blue-painted metal rails of the promenade, with the sand and shingle beach below. There's a boat anchored out at sea, with people swimming in the water close by, others on deck, and it reminds me of the day out on Jack's boat. The sea is crystal clear here, pebbles visible below the surface as the turquoise water washes over them. Further on, the beach soon gives way to the sea, gently crashing against the beach wall. The opposite side of the road is lined with apartments, cafés and restaurants with menu boards outside offering freshly caught fish.

I stop at a café and enjoy a cooling orange juice, and take in the glorious view of the beach across the road. After my refreshing drink, I continue walking and after a short distance, the sand appears once more, dotted with colourful parasols above people stretched out on sunbeds. The sun is beating down from the brilliant blue sky and I feel the burn on my legs once more as I walk.

Closer to the beach of Aghios Stefanos, olive trees line a long road, their leaves wafting in a gentle, welcome sea breeze. I breathe deeply as I walk, enjoying every second of being here.

Paying for a sunbed, I settle down with my beach things, and view the tiny island across the water, the blue roof of the white church standing out like a beacon. It doesn't look very far at all, I decide, peeling off my sundress, to reveal my swimming costume beneath. I take a sip from some bottled water, and stare out across the water to the island that feels almost within touching distance. There's a family next to me, and I ask if they are staying for the day, and if they would mind watching my things. They smile and say sure, as I head towards the water, feeling determined.

As I slide into the sea, it's thankfully nice and warm, and I start swimming, enjoying the feeling of the water as I make my way across to the island, where I can see several people standing close to the church. For a second, I realise it's the first exercise I have taken since my operation and hope I am not overdoing things, but I reassure myself as I recall the words of my doctor, who said gentle exercise is good for me. Is this gentle exercise?

I swim on, feeling the heat on my head, as a speedboat whizzes past, causing ripples in the water, and I catch my breath. Not really too far now; I concentrate on my breaststroke, which I've always done, although maybe front crawl would be a little faster. A thought occurs to me, that I won't be able to do any actual walking around the island, exploring its craggy terrain as I'm in my swimsuit. I'm not even wearing any swimming shoes, so it would appear I will have to swim over, rest for a while near the rocks, before swimming back. I'm cursing myself for not putting some thin shorts over my swimsuit, and maybe wearing swim shoes, as I can see it's very rocky. Apparently, people swim across here and ring the bell of the church from outside, before wandering round.

It's not far now, and I think maybe I can at least do that with one last push, when I suddenly feel a searing pain in my calf. I catch my breath as a gripping cramp overwhelms me and I am barely able to move. For a second, I go under, swallowing a little of the salty water and come up coughing. I steady my breathing and try to keep calm, flipping onto my back to float, but the pain in my leg is almost disabling. I wonder whether or not I'm imagining things, but a second later there's no mistake. Someone is calling my name.

Thankfully, the cramping begins to subside, but my leg does feel a little sore. I'm taking it easy, concentrating on my breathing, when out of nowhere, a small speedboat appears beside me. I look up and to my utter surprise, it's Georgios.

'Georgios! What are you doing here?' I splutter, hardly able to believe my eyes.

'I was at the beach,' he replies. 'Thought I'd take a speedboat out for a spin. Are you okay?'

'Yes, I'm fine. It isn't far.' I'm going to make it to the little island if it kills me. I don't need rescuing like some damsel in distress.

'You can drive me back if you like though,' I say casually. 'Seeing as you're here.'

'Of course. Are you sure you don't want to get in the boat now?'

'Positive.'

I swim alongside the boat, pushing forward and praying my leg doesn't cramp again. Thankfully, a few minutes later, I pull myself up onto the rocks on Kastri, aware that I'm dressed only in a swimsuit. Georgios offers me a huge yellow beach towel, which I gratefully wrap myself in. The area is a little rocky and I don't fancy walking around barefoot, but luckily the little church is so close that I manage to negotiate some flat rocks and ring the bell. I'm acutely aware of Georgios watching me as I return and climb into the boat, thankful to be covered up.

'Do you want to come back and have a proper look around? Maybe when you're wearing some clothes.'

'Could do. Although I don't think there's much to see. I'm

glad I got to ring the bell though. Anyway, what are you doing here? I thought you were meant to be writing all day?'

'A slight change of plan,' he says, starting the engine up and turning the boat around in the direction of the beach. 'I needed to head this way to run an errand for my grandfather, so whilst I was in the area, I thought I would check out the beach,' he says, a little unconvincingly.

'Really?'

'Yes, really. Although, okay, maybe I was hoping to run into you. Maybe I was a little concerned that you were planning on swimming to the island. You did mention that you haven't done any exercise in a while. And I know you have only recently been recuperating.'

He came here in case I got into trouble in the water?

'Well, as you can see, I'm perfectly fine. You don't need to worry about me. I would have swum back too, but I quite fancied the idea of a ride in a speedboat,' I say, as we speed along, the wind blowing my hair. It feels a little chilly and I wrap the towel around me tightly.

Georgios looks annoyingly gorgeous, as the wind ruffles his dark curly hair too. He's wearing sunglasses and a black T-shirt with denim shorts, an expensive-looking black watch on his wrist, replacing his usual leather bracelet. He suits being behind the wheel of the boat, and I find myself thinking that he wouldn't look out of place in an action movie. Not that I would ever tell him that.

'Now this is something you could definitely write about in your book,' I suggest. 'The heroine is given a lift to the beach by a sexy guy in a speedboat.'

Why did I use the word sexy?

'Is that what you think I am?' He turns to me and smiles a broad smile.

'No, I mean, it's fiction, right? I'm just saying some attractive guy rocks up, that's all.' My face is burning as hot on the sun. What on earth am I saying?

'Attractive *and* sexy.' He's laughing now and I want the ground – or should I say the water – to swallow me up.

I'm grateful when a couple of minutes later, he has anchored the boat and we stroll along the beach, where I thank the couple keeping an eye on my belongings and slip a sundress over my head, and pick up my straw hat.

'Do you fancy a walk along the beach?' I ask, placing my sunhat on.

'Sure. Actually, are you hungry?' he asks. 'It's about coming up to lunchtime.' He glances at his watch.

'I could eat something, I suppose. It feels like ages since breakfast.'

We walk slightly away from the main drag of the beach, in the direction of some ancient ruins. The section of the beach alongside it looks much quieter, with only one or two cafés overlooking the water. Soon enough we have arrived at the remains of the crumbling buildings that look out over the sparkling sea.

'The ruins of the Basilica Stefanos,' Georgios tells me. 'Built in the fourth and fifth century respectively; would you believe one was built on top of the other?'

'Really? How come?'

'The first was destroyed in an earthquake, so the second was built over it,' he tells me.

I look around at the ruins.

'Maybe you would like to have a wander around, after we've had something to eat?' he suggests.

'Yes, I think I would. It looks really interesting.'

I wonder if Chloe has been here with her camera? It's another place I must tell her about when we return to the hotel later.

Soon enough, we're sat at a restaurant with white walls and

green wicker chairs, dining on the most delicious seafood risotto and sipping ice-cold water.

'Thanks for this, Georgios, what a beautiful spot.' I glance around at some small colourful fishing boats, their redundant nets close by and old men sat on benches chatting to each other. 'And thanks for thinking about me today.'

'No problem. As I say, maybe I was hoping I would run into you.'

I'm a bit confused about his hot and cold behaviour, so I decide to be brave and ask him a question.

'Why were you hoping to run into me?' I ask, looking him straight in the eye.

He looks surprised for a minute.

'Because I like your company, Orla. I really like *you*.'

'Do you? Because sometimes you have a funny way of showing it. Sometimes you practically ignore me,' I tell him truthfully.

'I'm sorry.' He looks at me with those gorgeous brown eyes. 'I guess I have been a little preoccupied with the book. But it's true, I do like spending time with you.' He pauses for a moment. 'But maybe I've been unsure about growing close to someone who is only going to be here for a short time.'

He feels he's growing close to me? Am I growing close to him?

'I enjoy your company too,' I tell him honestly. 'And let's not think about how long I'm going to be here; nothing is set in stone. Let's just enjoy today, shall we?'

'Sounds good.' He smiles, and when he reaches across the table and squeezes my hand, I let it linger there for a minute.

We finish our delicious meal, and take the short walk back to the ruins, adjacent to the café. Walking around the ancient monuments, I'm surprised at how deserted it is, as most people appear to be sat beneath sunshades on the beach, reading or splashing about in the water, which is probably wise as the sun is really getting up at the hottest part of the day. There are some stone columns and remnants of mosaic floors as well as stone archways covered in moss. Georgios tells me a little more about the history of the church as we walk, which is useful as there is an absence of information boards.

A short while later, we sit down on some well-preserved steps, and just gaze out across the sparkling blue sea.

'Ah, it's just so gorgeous here, isn't it? So peaceful.' I sigh with pleasure.

Georgios points to some tiny islands in the distance, telling me his grandfather used to take him there sea fishing when he was a young boy. 'Although my sister was always better at sea fishing than I was,' he admits. 'I preferred messing about on the rocks looking for creatures, or scouring the beach for sea glass.'

'Sounds amazing. What lovely memories to have.'

'Do you have any brothers or sisters?' asks Georgios, and I feel a stab to the heart. I have to compose myself, almost not responding.

'I have a sister,' I eventually answer.

'That must be nice. Are you alike?'

'I don't know,' I tell him, avoiding his gaze and wonder why on earth I have just revealed this to a man I have only known for such a short time. 'I've never met her.' I turn to face him and although he tries to hide it, I can see the look of surprise on his face.

'I'm sorry to hear that. Is that from choice?' he asks me honestly.

'I've only recently found out about her. She lives here in Greece.'

It sounds shocking even to myself, as I say it out loud.

'She lives in Greece?'

'In Patmos, actually. It's one of the reasons I'm heading there.'

I find myself telling him about the letter I found when I was recovering from my operation at my family home.

'I remember as a young child Dad left the family home for a while.' I continue the story. 'My parents never spoke of that time again, as he returned eventually, but it was something I will never forget.' I pause for a minute, recalling the pain and confusion I felt. 'Anyway, it seems that during their separation, Dad met a woman. Or maybe she was the reason for the separation in the first place; I don't suppose I will ever know.'

Georgios listens intently, without interrupting me, so I find myself telling him the rest of the story.

'After a few weeks, Dad returned home. Mum vaguely explained his absence as Dad working somewhere far away, as to why he couldn't visit me. Of course, I now realise that wouldn't have been possible as he was here in Kos.'

'That must have been hard. How old were you?' he asks.

'I think it was harder to only find out the whole truth recently. I didn't really understand it at the time, I was so young. Almost six, I remember, because it was my birthday the week after he came home and I had a party. Mum agreed to give things another try. I don't know if he knew the woman he left behind was even pregnant.'

'Wow.' Georgios exhales. 'So, he actually met someone when he was here on a family holiday?'

'I guess so, but I'm not sure. Maybe Dad will tell me someday. Perhaps our little family unit wasn't as tight as I thought it was.'

'So, your father never told you about the letter?'

'No, he didn't, which, I won't lie, I was mad about. I might still be, a little. He may not have wanted to acknowledge his daughter here, but he had no right to deprive me of a sister.' I can hear the resentment in my own voice.

'Maybe he just needed time to process things,' suggests Georgios.

'I know. But I can't help thinking I would never have learned of her existence had I not been looking through old photos that day.' I choke back tears. 'She wanted a meeting with him, but it seems Dad didn't want to know.'

'So, you don't think he contacted her?'

'I'm not sure. I can only assume he ignored her request as, looking at the date on the letter, Mum was gravely ill at the time. It must have been so difficult for him, but he didn't want to upset Mum, knowing she wasn't long for this world. I do understand that, I suppose.'

'I can only imagine how that must make you feel,' he says gently.

'It makes me feel angry that he didn't tell me after Mum passed away,' I reply. 'Though I admit, I'm someone who has a tendency to avoid emotional issues, but this?' I sigh. 'She's my sister. All of my life I wanted a sister, and I can't help feeling such regret that we never had the chance to know each other when we were children,' I confess. 'But, of course, I know it isn't her fault. If this has taught me anything, it's that I'll never bury things or run away from them again.'

'People have to live with regret sometimes. But it wasn't your sister's fault. Children don't ask to be born.'

'Oh, Georgios, you're right, they don't. And I will meet her. I'm just worried she might turn me away,' I confess.

'I can't imagine why she would turn you away. She's reached out to your father. She must know there is a possibility he has another family. Anyway, how could she not fall in love with you?'

He edges closer to me on the wide step, and silently slides his arm around my waist. For a while we just sit and stare out across the water, neither of us feeling the need to speak.

'We have the BBQ at the hotel this evening,' I remind him a while later, even though I don't want the time here to end. 'So maybe we ought to be making a move,' I say.

'That's funny, I was just thinking of doing the same thing,' he tells me.

'What?'

'Making a move.' He's looking at me in a way that makes my heart skip a beat.

He leans in then and kisses me ever so softly on the lips, making every nerve in my body tingle, yet I know there is no point in longing for anything more as I'll be moving on tomorrow. Maybe he was right not to let his guard down and develop feelings for me.

'I hope you didn't mind me doing that,' he says.

'Of course not. It's just that...'

'I know.' He takes my hand in his. 'You will soon disappear, like some mythical mermaid of the sea.'

'Very poetic. I can see you are a writer.'

We sit quietly for a few moments, his hand still wrapped around mine, and I briefly consider abandoning all plans of heading to Patmos.

A while later, we stand and walk along the harbour front once more, passing shops, me commenting on something or other in a window as we make our way to the car park, which we have parked our respective cars in. Passing the blue railings along the beach, we make small talk as we walk, chatting about local beauty spots.

'See you back at the hotel,' I say, as we arrive at the car park and step into our cars.' And thanks again.'

'My pleasure. I've enjoyed this afternoon.' He smiles. 'It's been good getting to know you a little more.'

Driving home, I think about what has passed between us with a feeling of complete and utter confusion. I also wonder why Georgios came here today, when he told me he would be spending the day writing. I still can't believe he was concerned for my welfare, when I told him I would be swimming to Kastri, after I mentioned I hadn't been swimming in a while. I think about these things as I drive. I also think that maybe it's time I did a little more exercise, as my doctor has assured me it will be okay. I've been a little nervous of doing so, but I need to recover my fitness level. I used to walk miles through forests, before I began to feel ill, even enjoying strenuous hikes up hills in the Lake District.

My thoughts also turn to that gentle kiss, and how it made me feel. I can hardly wait for the BBQ this evening.

TWENTY-ONE

After showering, I change into a short black dress adorned with little coloured trumpets that I bought from a vintage store back home. I lightly backcomb my hair, add a silver cross around my neck and a slash of my trusty pink lipstick, in a rose blush shade.

Glancing out over the pool area from my balcony, I can hear Georgios tapping away on his computer, obviously making up some lost time after going out today and I hope his day in Kefalos hasn't set him back too much. The lights are on around the pool area, and the long wooden table is already set with chunky candles and glasses.

I can see Sophia putting finishing touches to a flower display at the centre of the table, before she threads some lights through a large shrub close to the pool. It's looking lovely already. Theo is stood next to the BBQ preparing the coals, the smell of gentle smoke, swirling in the air. I watch Sophia take a final glance around before she heads inside for something.

I nip inside and spray some perfume before I walk downstairs to the outside area and offer Sophia some help.

'Oh, thank you, Orla, but no, I am sure everything is under control. The meats have been marinating, the salad is ready. So,

I'm not sure why I feel a little nervous about this evening,' she says, twisting her necklace.

'Maybe because your gentleman friend will be here. He is still coming, isn't he?'

'Yes. In fact, I am expecting him any moment now.' She glances at her watch once more, before taking a sip from a glass of Prosecco at a nearby table and taking a final glance around the garden.

'You look lovely by the way,' I say. She's wearing a black wrap-over dress, her hair up and a gold necklace. 'Very elegant. I'm sure Yiannis will be very impressed.'

'Thank you, Orla, you look lovely too. Now then, napkins.' She pours me a drink from the bottle of Prosecco that's sat in an ice bucket on a small table with some champagne glasses, before dashing off to fetch the napkins.

Glancing around, I can see that Sophia really has done a lovely job in the garden. As well as the lights and candles, there are fresh displays of white flowers in colourful glazed pots placed around the fence, surrounding the beautifully manicured lawn.

With the coal on the BBQ now ready, Theo says he is just nipping out to collect his guest for the evening. Sophia continues to fuss around, patting her hair, checking her watch, taking a sip of Prosecco.

'Try and relax,' I tell her kindly. 'Everything looks wonderful.'

Just then, Brady and Iris appear, closely followed by Chloe and Amy, and Sophia offers them all a drink, taking her mind off her invited guest. A few minutes later, Theo reappears.

'I found someone outside looking for you,' he says, as a grey-haired, handsome gentleman steps towards Sophia and presents her with the bunch of flowers he is carrying.

'Oh, Yiannis. How lovely, thank you.' She beams.

Right behind Theo is an attractive blonde who looks to be

in her twenties, wearing a denim shirt-dress and high-heeled cork wedges.

'This is Christine,' says Theo and we all say hello.

Yiannis removes his smart jacket and offers to help, but Theo won't hear of it, and a while later there's an array of succulent steaks, and chicken skewers piled up on the table, alongside salads, dips and pitta breads. Sophia places a pile of plates on a nearby table, telling us all to help ourselves to the food.

The drinks flow, and finally Theo relaxes and joins his date, slipping his arm around her waist as we dine around the table, enjoying the delicious feast. I can't help thinking of Rose, although I do recall her saying that she and Theo had been friends for a long time, and mentioned they were just a casual thing. All the same, I'm shocked when Amy asks Christine how long they have been together, and she says a few months. I glance over at Theo, but I'm sure he's avoiding eye contact with me.

There's someone missing this evening, and I can't help but feel a stab of disappointment that Georgios is nowhere to be seen. I imagined a lovely, flirtatious evening, especially having enjoyed our time together so much at the beach today, but he obviously isn't feeling the same way. He was honest when he spoke of his reluctance to grow close as I'm travelling through. I can't believe I actually asked him what he was feeling.

I'm chatting to Chloe and Amy about their plans this evening, when out of the corner of my eye I see Georgios approach the table and I catch my breath. He looks effortlessly sexy, in a white T-shirt, a dark unbuttoned shirt thrown over the top and a pair of beige chinos.

'Kalispera, I am sorry I am late,' he says, taking a seat next to me. 'I was busy getting on with some work,' he explains.

'Do not worry, you are here now, and there is plenty of food left,' says Sophia, before she introduces her friend Yiannis and Theo's friend Christine, as he doesn't come forth to make the introduction. Georgios helps himself to some chicken and salad and Sophia hands him a cold beer.

Talk turns to holidays, and as the drinks flow and some music is played, everyone is in a jubilant mood, the evening really going with a swing.

'I hope you have all enjoyed the food,' says Sophia when people have eaten their fill. 'And now, Theo, will you demonstrate some Greek dancing?'

'I've been looking forward to this,' says Yiannis, and to my surprise he removes his jacket and rolls the sleeves up on his shirt. Sophia looks just as surprised as I do, her face a picture of joy. He'd clearly kept it a secret that he loves to dance.

The Greek music strikes up, and Theo places his arms around Christine's shoulders, and Yiannis around Sophia's. They demonstrate the steps as the rest of us clap along, enjoying the floor show. Then Theo suddenly grabs Chloe's hand and gets her up to dance. She is quickly joined by a delighted Amy, and we watch them dance. Theo goes through the steps once more as they watch carefully.

'Do you think you are ready?' he asks and they nod their heads, eager to get started.

Chloe and Amy really are very good at picking up the steps and a few minutes later, Brady and Iris have joined in the fun, moving along to the music, which has a slow rhythm to begin with. Theo gestures for me to join them too and I'm wondering what Georgios will do, given his hatred of dancing. I wonder about his reaction if they insist he joins in, anticipating a moody strop. I stand to join the others and, to my great shock, Georgios follows me.

We join the end of the line, and Georgios concentrates on the footwork, before quickly falling into step. Soon enough, the music is building to a fast crescendo and Brady quietly retires to the table, and takes a long drink of his beer. The rest of us throw our heads back and laugh like there's no tomorrow. At the end, we all give each other a round of applause. That really was a lot of fun.

'I really enjoyed that,' says Brady, when we all return to the table. I was amazed Georgios actually kept dancing until the music ended. 'But I can't dance at that speed, I'm not sure my old ticker is up to it,' he says, whilst Iris appeared to be having the time of her life, giggling as the music became faster and faster.

I still can't get over the fact that Georgios got up to dance, and wonder whether he may have thought about coming out of his comfort zone after all.

Brady strikes up a conversation with Georgios, talking about American football, politics and food.

'What a wonderful evening, Sophia,' I compliment our hostess, 'and Yiannis is such a great dancer! I don't know what I was expecting, although truthfully, I had an image of a somewhat strait-laced bank manager.'

'Do you think I would be interested in someone who never had a twinkle in their eye?' she says, pushing me playfully on the arm.

'No, I guess not.' I laugh. 'And I must say, you two look good together. I hope things work out between you.'

'Thank you, time will tell.'

We're chatting together, as Yiannis has joined in the conversation with Georgios and Brady.

'I'm not sure about Theo and Christine though,' Sophia says, watching her as she chats to Iris.

'What do you mean?' I ask.

'I have a feeling, maybe she is keener than he is,' says Sophia observantly, noting Theo on his phone. 'He is glued to that thing,' she continues, shaking her head.

I agree with Sophia and can't help thinking I would be less than pleased if a date of mine spent half of his evening glancing at his phone, especially if he had brought me home to meet his mother.

Chloe and Amy sneak off a while later to a late bar and as the evening winds down, and Yiannis bids us all goodnight, Georgios and I sit together and enjoy a quiet drink. Theo leaves with Christine, telling Sophia he will see her later.

'I was surprised you got up to dance, given how much you hate it,' I can't help commenting.

'Yes, but I was shown the steps. I'm okay following a routine. It's just freestyle kind of dancing, I'm so bad at it that I don't enjoy it.'

I'm definitely not going to mention stepping out of that comfort zone again.

'Have you had a productive day with your book?' I ask as I sip a chilled glass of water. I'm off to Patmos tomorrow and don't want to risk a hangover when I'm travelling.

'Very productive, actually. Things aren't going so well with the main character and her love interest though.' He twirls the stem of his wine glass.

'How so?'

'It's complicated. They are two totally different people, at least they seem to be. Deep down they are similar. They will realise that in the end though, and fall madly in love. I just haven't figured out how that's going to happen yet.'

'Real life isn't like it is in books and movies, is it? I'm sure everything will all fall neatly into place.'

Georgios shrugs. 'Maybe some people's relationship expectations are unreal.'

'Are you saying you ought to settle for someone you are not completely happy with? I definitely don't agree with that.'

'No, that's not what I'm saying at all. But we have to be prepared to love someone, despite their flaws. It's worth remembering that no one is perfect.' He takes a sip of his wine, waiting for my response.

I think about his words that hang in the air between us. No one is perfect. Maybe I've been a complete nightmare in the past, dashing off, growing bored quickly, never giving relationships a chance to really develop. There's no such thing as perfection, Georgios is right about that. So why is it that I can't seem to settle down? What will make me change and how will I know when I find it?

The sky is black, studded with stars and Georgios and I continue chatting after Sophia has said goodnight and retired to her bed, along with Brady and Iris.

'What time are you leaving tomorrow?' asks Georgios as the temperature has dropped a little and the air feels a little cooler.

'I'm catching a late morning sailing. I've agreed to drop the car at a Hertz rental here in Kos.'

'Have you got your travel-sick pills?' asks Georgios, smiling, and I cringe when I think of how the pirate cruise ended and I vomited on his shoes.

'No, but maybe that's not such a bad idea.'

I give a little shiver in the cooler air, and Georgios heads towards the bar and returns with a fleecy throw. He stands behind me and slides it gently around my shoulders.

'Thank you. How did you know where to find that?'

'I watched Sophia retrieve one the other evening for Iris.'

'I'm glad you noticed,' I say, snuggling into the soft blanket.

'I notice everything. I guess it's the writer in me, observing every detail about my surroundings, especially the people.' He regards me closely before he speaks. 'I'll miss you, Orla,' he says as he resumes his seat beside me.

'Will you?' I ask, my mind flitting to the gentle kiss we shared earlier today.

'Of course I will. I was just getting to know you, and off you go,' he says, before moving closer and taking hold of my hand. 'You really are a special person, Orla. I wish you were staying around a little longer, so I could get to know you more.'

'I don't think I'm so special, I—'

Before I can utter any more words, he has silenced me with a kiss, and my stomach does a somersault. It feels so wonderful and I want to stay in this moment forever, kissing this gorgeous man beneath the stars, maybe even making our way upstairs. Suddenly I break free from his embrace, my head spinning. There can be no point to this liaison, however wonderful it feels. Tomorrow I'll be heading off somewhere new, where I'm hoping to resolve something that has been weighing heavily on my mind and maybe even finding a new member of my family.

TWENTY-TWO

I rise early the next morning, and head across to the beach for an early morning yoga session to set me up for the day ahead. Once again, I marvel at the sight of the rising sun and inhale the sea air as the waves crash onto the shore. Does the sight of the breaking dawn on a beach ever get old? I can't help wondering whether even I would tire of such a place.

I had a fitful sleep last night, reliving that heart-stopping kiss, knowing Georgios was in the next bedroom, and wondering if he was thinking about me. Yet I'm aware that today I am moving on. Maybe that was why he was a perfect gentleman last night, not inviting me into his room, yet once more a part of me wishes he had done.

There are several more people at the class today, as word seems to be spreading about Theo's class. Rose is there in her usual spot. Limbering up.

'Rose, hi, I'm glad you are here, although I imagined you would be. I leave for Patmos later this morning. I didn't want to leave without saying goodbye.'

'Gosh, that's come around quickly,' she says as she straightens up after touching her toes with the ease of a much younger person. 'If you have time, we could have a smoothie after the session,' she suggests.

'Yes, I'd like that.'

I enjoy a marvellous yoga session; Theo really is a great teacher, whose lessons I know I will miss. I feel refreshed and energised when the session is over, ready to embrace the day ahead.

Rose and I stroll to a nearby beach bar and I order a strawberry smoothie, whilst Rose orders a coffee, before fumbling in her back pocket for a cigarette.

'Silly really, isn't it?' She stares at the cigarette in her hand. 'All that mindfulness and deep breathing, and here I am putting these toxins into my body.' She pulls a face. 'I've cut down massively though. Maybe five a day, usually with a drink or after a bite to eat. Probably a habit really,' she admits.

'Maybe you ought to get one of those fake ones from the joke shop you told me about after all.'

Rose laughs. 'Maybe I should.'

Talk turns to the previous evening, and I tell Rose all about the BBQ at the hotel.

'It was a lot of fun. And Georgios actually got up to dance, which he normally hates.'

'Was Theo there?' asks Rose, blowing a plume of smoke away from the table.

'Yes, he was.'

'Was he alone?' she asks casually.

I'm not going to lie to Rose.

'No, he brought someone along, actually. A girl called Christine.'

'That's his girlfriend.' Rose sighs. 'Although, he obviously doesn't treat her very well. I don't know what you must think of me, knowing that we slept together.'

'I would never judge you, Rose,' I say genuinely. 'Although,

I'd say having feelings for a guy like Theo would be a big mistake.' I take a sip of my tasty strawberry smoothie.

'It would,' she admits. 'So luckily, I don't have those kinds of feelings for him, which makes it sound even worse, but I didn't know he had a girlfriend, truly. He kind of told me they were on and off and I believed they were having a break. As I say, I've known Theo for a while but sleeping with him was a huge mistake.' She sighs.

'We all make mistakes. At least there's no awkwardness between you, as you still attend his classes.'

'I know. Annoyingly, I don't think I could find a better teacher,' she admits, reaching for her coffee.

I hug Rose goodbye before I head back to the hotel for a final breakfast. She asks for my phone and taps her number into it, saying maybe we could meet for coffee some time to catch up, and I realise I would really like that.

It's a little after eight o'clock when I return to the hotel and I'm surprised to find Chloe and Amy tucking into breakfast, with Brady and Iris.

'You two are up early?' I comment to the girls.

'I know,' says Chloe. 'We only have a few days left of our holiday, so we've decided we want to make the most of every minute. We're taking inspiration from Brady and Iris and are off on the Three Island tour later. Especially as you said it was the highlight of your stay, didn't you?'

'Oh, it was,' replies Iris with a smile. 'Seeing those dolphins did it for me.'

We have a lingering breakfast, and before Brady and Iris head off, Iris invites me to come and stay if I'm ever in Texas. She also tells me she is on Facebook, and will send me a friend request. Georgios hasn't appeared for breakfast yet, so the girls and I have a little chat about the previous evening. They tell me they went for a dance at Mambo's.

'And,' squeals Chloe excitedly, 'I have a date with Jack tomorrow evening.'

'You do? Ah, I knew there was an attraction between you two.' I feel happy for her, although I hope she doesn't get hurt, given Jack's supposed reputation with the ladies.

'Tell her the rest, Chloe,' urges Amy.

'It turns out that Jack's not a dirty dog after all. I had a few drinks, and kind of plucked up the courage to mention what Theo had said about him.'

'Really? And what did he have to say?'

'He said Theo had made the whole thing up. It turns out Jack had a relationship with one of Theo's ex-girlfriends, when it was well and truly over between them, of course. Anyway, Theo was really hurt as he thought he would have a future with the girl in question. Jack told us that Theo has bad-mouthed him ever since, warning girls off, saying he had an affair with his girlfriend, which Jack swears he didn't. He really set out to ruin his reputation, even going so far as to recommend rival boat trips to guests staying at the hotel.'

'Gosh, I'm shocked Theo would behave in such a way. He must have been pretty cut up over his girlfriend, but even so, it's a pretty childish thing to do.'

And given Theo's apparent disregard for his current girl-friend, I think he's the one women ought to be warned about.

'Exactly. I never could believe Jack was the type of bloke Theo described.'

'I know, me neither, if I'm honest. Jack's such a nice guy, it just didn't ring true.'

'It's a kind of double date too,' Amy confides, with a beaming smile. 'Although, I'm not thinking of it in a romantic way. Mike was at Mambo's last night too, and just kind of said the four of us should meet up together for dinner. Chatting to him I discovered he's actually interested in the history of the island and said he'd take me on a private tour on his day off.'

'Sounds lovely. I hope you all have the best time. And good luck with your studies.' I give them a hug, and once again we swap numbers and promise to keep in touch via social media, Instagram being their preferred platform.

A while later, I head upstairs to pack and I'm surprised that Georgios isn't on his balcony. In fact, his patio door is closed. I know he's up against it with his book, so perhaps he's spending the day inside writing. Even so, I kind of thought we might have enjoyed a final breakfast together and feel a tiny bit disappointed that he hasn't even bothered to say goodbye.

TWENTY-THREE

'It has been wonderful having you here, Orla.' Sophia crushes me in a hug. 'And next year, there may be two more bedrooms if you decide to return. The upstairs one will give a great sea view; I will reserve it for you, if you would like.'

'Oh, that sounds wonderful, Sophia. Please let me know when the extension is completed. If I return to Kos there is nowhere else I would consider staying.'

Theo gives me a hug and says he will miss me at the yoga classes.

'I'll miss your classes too,' I tell him. 'Although Rose will still be there, and I know she's a good friend.' I then whisper out of earshot of Sophia, 'Although maybe you ought to make sure she stays just a friend. People can get hurt.'

He actually looks a little embarrassed, and stares down at his shoes.

'I know. Maybe I haven't been the best version of myself lately,' he says as Sophia walks away to answer the phone inside. 'But I will be. I've ended things with Christine; it isn't fair on her if I can't fully commit. I'm going to take some time out, maybe steer clear of relationships for a while. I will be too busy at the hotel anyway when work begins on the extension.'

'And if you don't mind me saying, maybe you ought to think twice about bad-mouthing Jack.'

He holds his hands up. 'I will. I did think that he actually stole my girlfriend, but I think differently now. I realise you cannot steal someone away from a happy relationship. She had a mind of her own.'

'Well, I really hope you work things out. You're not a bad person, Theo; be kind to yourself.'

'Thank you, Orla. You are a wise woman.'

'Hmm. Maybe not as wise as you think. By the way, have you seen Georgios this morning?' I ask him.

'No, actually. He hasn't taken breakfast in his room either. Maybe he's sleeping in?'

It's just after ten o'clock, so I can't imagine he would still be sleeping. Then again, he may have been awake half the night getting on with his writing, so I guess it's possible.

Upstairs, I pack the last of my things, intending to knock at Georgios' door before I depart, but something inside stops me from doing so. He knew I would be leaving today, so he clearly doesn't feel the need to say a final goodbye. And, if I'm honest, I realise it's probably for the best.

I drop my car off at a local car rental, then take a taxi down to the busy harbour to board the boat to Patmos. There are a few market stalls near the port and as I recall Tim asking for a jar of good olives, I purchase some from a local grower. I buy a jar of mountain honey too, along with a bottle of thyme-scented virgin olive oil.

I have just over half an hour to wait for the boat, so I pass the time by reading my book on a nearby bench in a shelter. I had such a wonderful time in Kos. Although it does surprise me a little that Georgios wasn't around this morning to say goodbye, especially as he knew I was sailing today. I think of last night and the wonderful chat we had in the candlelight, when the others had gone to bed, and the thoughtful way he fetched me a blanket when I was a little cold, and gently draped it over my shoulders. His actions were filled with such kindness and tenderness, that I can't help feeling confused over his absence this morning. And then there was that kiss. A real, meaningful kiss this time, that sent thrills through my whole body. Perhaps he regretted it, which explains why he wasn't around this morning, yet something feels unfinished between us. It feels strange to be sailing off into the distance, but there is little I can do about it now. I try hard to recall the last thing he said to me, as I try to fathom his non-appearance at breakfast. With a heavy heart, I realise it was along the lines of wishing me a safe onward journey, so perhaps he never felt the need to say it again this morning. All the same, I'm surprised by how completely disheartened I feel.

Boarding the boat a while later, I immerse myself in my book, pausing to take in the view of the surrounding area. Sunshine is dancing on the water and clusters of white houses cling to hills in the background. It isn't long before the hills of Patmos are stretched out ahead, beckoning us towards them.

'I wish I could stay here forever.' An Englishwoman, her dark hair tied back in a band and wearing a long white dress with a peach cardigan thrown over, sighs as she glances out across the water.

'I know it's beautiful. Are you on holiday here?' I ask.

'I'm staying in Kos,' she tells me. 'I've been looking forward to making this sail to Patmos. I want to visit the cave. Is that where you're heading?' she asks brightly.

'I will be visiting it, yes, although I'm actually staying on Patmos for a few days.'

'Oh, that sounds lovely.' She smiles. 'I'm going to light a

candle in the cave and say a prayer for my elderly neighbour; she's been very depressed since her husband died.' She looks out across the sea once more, lost in her thoughts for a moment. 'There are quite a few activities for pensioners in our local area, but she hasn't got the heart to go to them. She does come to my place for tea though and I take her shopping sometimes.'

I can't help thinking how people often pray for miracles to help someone walk, or maybe fight a disease, but how many people pray to be cured of depression, I wonder?

'She's lucky to have a neighbour like you.' I smile. 'Everyone needs someone to talk to; loneliness is a terrible thing.'

'Thanks. And you're right, loneliness must be awful. Are you here on your own then?' she asks and I smile to myself, thinking how we never mind telling other women that we're travelling alone. Maybe she thinks I'm lonely, but nothing could be further from the truth.

'I am. I'm heading somewhere else after this, which might be Samos, or maybe I will head straight to Rhodes and fly home. I haven't quite decided yet.'

'Ooh, so you're the adventurous type, are you?'

'I guess I am. I have travelled around a bit. But my love of Greece began as a child.'

We chat about holidays, and she tells me she discovered Greece four years ago, after booking a trip here on impulse.

'It was the first time I'd been anywhere on my own, and the bravest thing I've done in my entire life, but I just thought sod it,' she reveals. 'My husband wasn't interested in going abroad, said he didn't like the sound of the food, and the sun brought him out in a rash. Twenty years I went along with it, going no further than Cornwall in September, when it wasn't too hot. Then do you know what he goes and does?'

'No.' I shake my head.

'He bloody leaves me. Runs off with someone he worked with, and within a few months they'd gone on holiday to Spain.

I can't tell you how angry I was. All those years and he would never go abroad with me.' She shakes her head.

'That must have hurt.'

'Oh, it did. But it also spurred me on not to waste another second of my life. I came to Greece on a singles holiday four years ago and have been coming twice a year ever since. I've made some lovely friends in Kos.'

'Well, good for you, I'm pleased you are getting on with your life.'

'My ex did me a favour.' She smiles. 'And for the record, his romance with the workmate didn't last. Classic midlife crisis, I'd say.'

We sail on beneath the baking hot sun, sipping cold drinks and chatting, when I hear my phone ringing in my bag. For some reason, I think it might be Georgios and I excitedly retrieve it, although I suddenly realise that he never asked me for my number. Pulling my phone from my bag, I can see it's a video call on Messenger and when I answer it's the gang from Potters.

'Orla, hi!' My work friends are all huddled around a desk, waving furiously at the camera.

'Oh, my goodness, hi everyone.' I wave at my friends and feel a sudden rush of affection.

'How's the holiday going?' asks Tim, who's at the centre of the huddle, Polly alongside him, smiling.

'It's wonderful. Want to take a look where I am right now?'

I turn my phone to landscape and pan it around, showing them the boat, the sparkling sea and the glorious view beyond.

'Okay, that's enough,' Tim says, laughing. 'It looks wonderful, Orla, I'm glad you're having a good time, you deserve it.'

'Thanks, guys.'

We chat for a few minutes, as I tell them how much I enjoyed Kos and that I'm now heading for Patmos. Soon, the rest of the gang disappear back to their desks, and Polly takes her phone to the office to continue the chat for a little longer.

'How are things going with Tim?' I ask.

'Really good.' She smiles brightly. 'He's so lovely. And I'm happy to say that we share a love of walking. We headed up to the Lake District at the weekend.'

'Ooh lovely, did you stay over somewhere?'

'No, actually, it was just a day trip. We haven't taken that step yet, as I don't want to rush into anything.'

'I suppose that's sensible,' I agree. 'Especially as you work together.'

I consider telling Polly all about the kiss with Georgios but stop myself. What would be the point of talking about something that clearly isn't going to develop? And there is so much else I have on my mind that I haven't told her. The closer my trip to Patmos comes, the more what my time on the island could bring has been weighing on me. I will need to address so much when I eventually head home that, for now, I just want to keep this to myself.

Finishing the call, I see we are almost at the Port of Patmos, as the sight of a large monastery, that looks more like a fortress, stands proud over the island. A man at the harbour side guides our boat in and soon we are moored up and disembarking. I stare at the hills that rise up into the distance, and the houses that are dotted about on the rugged and, in places, slightly barren-looking landscape. I say goodbye to the English lady I was chatting to and wish her well.

'Thanks, love. Enjoy your stay here,' she says as she joins the throng of tourists heading towards an awaiting minibus.

Many of the boat people are day trippers who come here primarily for the tour of the cave and a lunch stop on an organised tour.

I take a taxi from the harbour at Skala to my rented apartment, which is in Chora, at the top of a slightly steep hill. I arrive at a pale-blue painted townhouse of which I have rented the whole of the upper floor. Once inside, I glance around the spacious lounge, with beautiful terracotta walls and coloured glass lamps that give it a Moroccan feel. A large sofa has a cream throw and orange cushions, overlooked by a small kitchen with blue-painted wooden doors. There's a large, airy bedroom with an en-suite shower; the bedroom leads out onto a small balcony that gives a magnificent view of the sea and the mountains. I take a deep breath as I look out across the hills to the sea beyond.

After I've unpacked a few things, I take the letter from my handbag, and my stomach turns over with nerves. What if Sula isn't at home when I call at her house? I wanted to speak to her first, but part of the phone number has been smudged away, although the address remains intact.

I decide to take a stroll around the area and find a taverna for a coffee and something to eat. It's still busy down at the harbour front, as people are boarding a ferry to Kos. I'm almost tempted to buy a ticket and head back across the water to speak to Georgios, although I know I'm probably procrastinating on the issue I have to address here on Patmos.

Heading off to do some shopping, I wander the backstreets, passing a small bakery and, flanked by houses, a white church with its bell pealing out across the square. Two elderly ladies are sat on a bench in the cobbled square, chatting as they watch over two young children playing close by. Walking on, I notice a group of tourists following a tour guide who is holding his umbrella aloft as people gather around him. He is speaking in French, and describing an old white building with white, rough stone walls. Making out one or two of his words, I believe it is a school that was built in the seventeen hundreds.

After I've finished exploring the maze of streets, it's late afternoon, so I head home to shower and read on the small balcony of my apartment.

It's quite a walk back uphill, but every now and then, I stop to admire the spectacular view of the sparkling sea below. At a small supermarket, not far from my apartment, I purchase a bottle of wine, bread, cheeses, and the ingredients for a Greek salad. This evening I am looking forward to taking dinner on my balcony and watching the sun go down. Tomorrow I will think of other more serious issues.

TWENTY-FOUR

I wake early the next morning, taking coffee on the balcony outside and watching the sunrise over the sea. It's another gorgeous day here and I look forward to exploring the island, first stop being to make my way to the Cave of John the Apostle. Before I head out, I will spend the morning doing a little reading of another book I packed, after finally finishing the one set in the Scottish castle, which I really enjoyed. I think the Scottish Highlands may now be on my future travel list.

Later, I investigate Patmos, stopping for a coffee here and there and browsing some gift shops. It's getting on for lunchtime when I go in search of the cave, following a tourist sign. I walk along a quiet backstreet, and see a notice on a wall with directions to the Baptist cave. It's a little after twelve thirty, and I'm disappointed to find that the cave has closed for the morning and only opens again at four o'clock. Obviously the day trippers must have visited whilst I was exploring the area. I head down to the harbour front at Skala to pass some time, and wander around the shops near the beach.

Down at Skala Harbour, I find a map of walking trails in a tourist shop, so armed with a bottle of water and already wearing a pair of trainers, I set off for a walk. The locals here are some of the most hospitable I have ever met and greet me with a wide smile and a *kalispera* whenever I encounter them.

Heading away from the harbour, I begin down some cobbled streets that soon give way to rugged landscape, some of the paths a little overgrown. Every now and then as I ascend, I stop to look at the stunning view below. I see churches spread on the hillside and windmills in the far distance. I follow a slightly obscured trail and find myself walking through a goat pasture, having to open and close gates to prevent the animals escaping. According to my map, this is the archaeological site of Kastelli. Turning a corner, I spot some ruins of a village, one or two doorways still intact, although mainly it's a jumble of bricks and shards of pottery. The view from here is spectacular, and I take a deep breath and soak in the beauty of the view that stretches out below.

It's just so peaceful here, in complete contrast to the busy island of Kos, and is a haven for walkers even though some of the paths are a little ill-defined, but that just adds to its rugged beauty. The island shows a real glimpse of the real Greece.

I make my descent and, spotting a sign for Chora, I leave the path that leads down towards Skala and make my way back to my apartment.

There's a narrow street of just six houses not far from where I am staying, and I read the sign on the street. It's the one. From the address on the letter. The reason I'm here on Patmos. I stand and just stare at the red-painted front door, but I'm not going to knock. Not today. I catch my breath as a front door opens, but it's the one next door, from which an elderly man emerges. Tomorrow. I will definitely return tomorrow.

I can feel the heat on my arms when I arrive at my apartment and smooth some cooling aftersun into my skin once I'm inside. I check my phone, which I'd forgotten to take out with me as it was charging, but there are no messages. Not that I was really expecting any.

An hour later, I set off for the cave and this time, there is a crowd assembled outside. I've come prepared, wearing a long sundress, and I respectfully drape a scarf around my head. After standing outside for just a few minutes, a man dressed in a pale-blue shirt and dark trousers unlocks the door and beckons us forward.

Above the entrance to the cave is a mosaic depicting Prochoros writing beside St John the disciple, supposedly translating his visions into script.

After descending a flight of grey stone steps, I step inside the cave and the first things I notice are the sculptures and paintings that adorn the walls, along with faded frescoes on the ceiling.

It's cool inside the cave, a welcome respite from the heat outside, and an atmosphere that is so silent that it is almost eerie, despite the visitors who are milling around. There are unlit candles in sconces and some of the pilgrims step forward and light one, their heads bent in silent prayer. In a corner there is a wooden chair, said to be the very place where John did his writings.

It doesn't take long to explore the cave, although I find myself in no rush to emerge back outside into the street, enjoying the moving experience. I'm surprised. It's hard to imagine John the Apostle sitting here, all those years ago writing about such an important biblical story as the Apocalypse, recorded in the Book of Revelation, and I feel honoured to be here. Some people have cast doubt about this being the actual place he did the writings, but as there is evidence that John did live on Patmos, after being exiled from Ephesus, I like to think I may have walked in his footsteps.

Later that evening, I come across the watercolour pencils and sketchpad I bought in Kos and take it outside, feeling inspired by my explorations. I sketch the outline of the hills and sea below, just as a bird flies across the horizon. I'd forgotten just how soothing sketching is, and to my surprise two hours fly by as I concentrate on the picture, smudging colours and dipping my pencil lightly into some water.

I place my little picture on the table inside, which although not a masterpiece, I think has really captured the view from the balcony and I feel rather pleased with myself. How often do we abandon our talents as we are too busy with our lives, or at least never really take the time out to nurture them? Maybe I'm only just realising that.

The cave visit has brought out something spiritual in me, as I find myself thinking about life and how fragile it is. I think about my own mortality, and how I might have endured the headaches and blurred vision for a lot longer, being someone who rarely visits a doctor, had I not collapsed that day in front of my work family. I might have continued swallowing painkillers and putting things down to too much screen time and dread to think of what might have happened if I had. Collapsing at work may have been meant to be, my colleagues seeking medical attention that I might have shrugged off at home. I wonder if I might even be here had my friends not come to the rescue. I swallow down a lump in my throat when I think of all these things, grateful to be here living my life and seeing such beautiful places. I also find myself thinking of Georgios and his comments about me running away from issues I can't face. I know there is definitely something I have to face here though.

After sitting with my thoughts for a while, I decide to head out for another walk before finding somewhere for dinner.

I wander the streets in the village of Chora, which flourished during the seventeenth century, passing through the tiny backstreets, their white walls hung with pretty pink bougainvillea seen throughout Greece. I walk between some beautiful tall houses, with pretty window boxes and carvings above heavy wooden doors. These houses were originally built by wealthy merchants and sea captains of the time.

Walking on, I come across a sign on a white wall advertising a rooftop restaurant nearby, so I follow the arrow and shortly I am escorted upstairs to a terrace that looks out beyond the houses and mountains and gives a glimpse of the sea beyond. The terrace is strung with white fairy lights, and a handful of the dozen or so tables are occupied.

I dine on the most delicious fried goat's cheese, summer salad and meatballs in a tomato sauce, before finishing with a delicious aged drink called *tsipouro*, which gives me a warm and mellow feeling inside. Sitting here, I glance down at the village below, where all the twinkling lights have come on and it looks stunningly beautiful. Stepping out of the restaurant, it's almost ten o'clock and I feel reassured that the backstreets are well lit, and a few women are sat outside houses on chairs chatting in the warm evening. As I walk on, it feels a little isolated and as I turn a corner, I can feel someone's presence behind me.

'*Kalispera.*' An elderly man doffs his cap and smiles as he walks ahead of me. I think it might be the man I saw today, emerging from the doorway of the house.

'*Kalispera,*' I say, returning the smile. I remind myself that it's very safe walking through the village, as are most places in Greece.

I continue my walk through the narrow streets, passing the occasional bar and café, their yellow lights shining out across the cobbles and leading the way. Cats prowling the quiet streets cross my path and bar owners greet me with a *kalispera*, as they stand in doorways and invite me inside for a drink. I politely decline on this occasion, but as there is one very close to the apartment I'm renting, I may pop out another evening for a nightcap.

I enter my own accommodation, accessed by a staircase at

the side of the house, and stifle a yawn as tiredness sweeps over me. I feel immediately at ease in this lovely, relaxing space, that I might have furnished myself, as I like the décor so much. I lie down on the large double bed and stretch out like a starfish. It's been a wonderful day here in Patmos and I'm looking forward to what adventures lie ahead. As much as I am excited thinking about what tomorrow could bring, I'm also a bundle of nerves – after all this planning and waiting, I hope it all goes well. And that I can build up the courage to knock on that red door.

TWENTY-FIVE

My downstairs neighbours are stepping out into the bright sunshine just as I reach the bottom of the stairs.

'*Kalimera*,' I say, determined to practise my Greek.

'*Kalimera*,' says the woman, who actually looks Scandinavian.

I head downhill a little and take a seat at an outdoor café, which gives a distant glimpse of the sea from its elevated terrace.

I get chatting to an English couple on the next table and tell them that I've been to Kos, and will be heading to Samos in a few days' time.

'How exciting,' says the lady, who tells me she and her husband have retired and are also travelling. 'I'm not sure I would ever have had the courage to do something like that at your age, alone. Good for you.'

I think about her remark as I sip some freshly squeezed orange juice. I've never thought of myself as courageous before, but I guess travelling alone is not something everyone might be comfortable with.

After tucking into a tasty omelette, I glance down at the

harbour. There's another tourist boat approaching, as well as several small speedboats out on the water enjoying the wonderful weather. The small shingle and sand beach has families spending the day together, splashing about in the water or eating from picnic baskets.

The couple tell me they will be heading up to the monastery shortly in their hire car and say I am welcome to join them.

'That's really kind,' I reply. 'And I was actually thinking of visiting the monastery, but maybe I will walk up, at my own pace.'

I'm aware of trying to improve my fitness.

'I probably would myself, if I was ten years younger,' the woman says with a smile. 'Maybe see you there.'

When the friendly couple leave, I order myself a coffee so I can continue enjoying the breath-taking view for a little while longer. It's just so peaceful sitting here, drinking coffee in the sunshine and watching the world go by. I feel so blessed to have met some lovely people on this journey, while also savouring the time I spend alone.

I can hardly believe I am here to look up my sister. Although technically a half-sister, it doesn't matter to me. There is someone out there who shares the same genes as me and I feel I owe it to both of us to at least meet each other. For a while, I thought about letting sleeping dogs lie, wondering if there would be any point to our meeting, but I knew that I would never rest until we had. And hadn't she reached out by writing the letter to our father?

I'm about to leave, when a parade passes by, the sound of a banging drum heralding the start of the procession of people dressed up in brightly coloured outfits passing through the street heading towards the harbour. There's a float easing its way downhill with a heavily made-up lady, adorned with flow-

ers, sitting on a chair. A stilt walker walks behind, followed by
an acrobat performing somersaults.

I suddenly think of Pascha. He was someone I really liked,
but when the relationship began to get serious, I backed off. I
told him it would never work as he was travelling all over the
country with the circus, and I'd grown tired of the job by then.
Pascha insisted he would give it all up in a heartbeat, but I told
him he would be miserable if he did that, hiding my fear behind
his love of circus life. I suppress a feeling of guilt when I think
of how I might have hurt people in the quest for a perfect relationship. Maybe true love isn't like that. Maybe love is just love,
and can overcome any obstacles.

Once the road is clear again, I begin the ascent uphill, the
majestic monastery looming over the streets, beckoning me
towards it as I approach. Several groups of people pass me on
the way down, chatting and sipping water.

Climbing further, I see a monk dressed in black with a long
beard and a dark hat, walking with a heavily laden donkey. He
bows his head and smiles as I walk past. As I carry on I see
several more monks, clearly a familiar sight in the village,
engaging with tourists and locals – unlike some monasteries
where the monks are often unseen, living behind closed doors.
There is a flour mill and garden for growing vegetables and the
monks work hard to provide for themselves.

Arriving at the monastery, I stand and stare at the ancient
building and can't help being transported back in time. At the
top of the church is a tower with three bells, the village below
crowned by the imposing monastery walls.

Inside, I marvel at the old paintings covering the ceiling of
the chapel, taking in the smell of polished wood and a faint smell
of incense. Outside, I stroll around a cobbled courtyard that has a
round stone structure at the centre that looks like a well. I consult
a leaflet I picked up and see that it is actually a very large jar,

once used to store wine. These days it is used to store holy water. Behind the well are four arched colonnades, proudly standing in front of walls displaying seventeenth-century paintings depicting different miracles performed by St John the Divine. It's all so magnificent I could stay here all day, just drinking it in.

It's good to see a monastery bustling with activity, with monks living there and interacting with the local community. The beauty of the monastery is testament to the determination of the monks to keep the artistic murals and artefacts in good condition, for the pleasure of the tourists. In fact, during my visit, two art experts are actually at work gently cleaning an old painting, bringing the red and rust colours to life and revealing the vibrant shades that had previously been covered in a film of dust.

I step inside the main chapel, richly decorated with dark panels adorned with gold and brocade wall hangings depicting various biblical scenes. There are intricate wooden carvings everywhere and silver lanterns suspended from the ceiling. After I've had a good look around the beautiful building, I walk outside into the bright sunshine once more, the dazzling white walls of the building in complete contrast to the dark interior I have just come from.

The couple from the café are sitting beneath a tree sipping water from a bottle.

'Hi, love, so you made it up then?' says the lady.

'Oh, hi. Yes, I did. It was a nice walk, actually. I even saw a donkey. It really is like stepping back in time, isn't it?'

'Oh, it is. Did you see the street parade too? Not sure what that was about.' She laughs.

'I think it was to do with a religious day, from what I over-heard someone say,' I tell her. 'Well, enjoy the rest of your holiday.' I wave goodbye, ready for the walk down the hill.

Presently, I pass the road of the address on the letter, and once more my nerve fails me as I head back to my rented accommodation.

After a while, feeling restless, I head out into the sunshine when I hear a voice behind me.

'Alright, fancy meeting you here?'

It takes me a minute to recognise the good-looking bloke who is stood in front of me smiling.

'It's Dean. We sat together on the plane,' he says, at exactly the same moment I remove my sunglasses and recognition dawns.

'Dean, hi! Sorry, you were in the shadow of a tree and what with the sunglasses, I didn't recognise you for a minute.'

'That's okay. Maybe it's the tan.' He smiles, stretching his arm out. 'I look like a local now, don't I?' He laughs.

With his dark hair and deep tan, he actually could pass for a Greek citizen.

'Your tan is indeed impressive.' I smile. 'So how are you? Is your holiday going well?'

'Brilliant. I didn't realise how stressed out I was when I first arrived in Kos, but it actually took a few days for me to unwind. I was obsessively checking my business website, even though my daughter is handling things in my absence.'

'I imagine it's hard to switch off when you run your own business.'

I recall Dean telling me all about his new online venture when we were on the plane and how he had previously lost his job.

'It is. My daughter thinks I'm a control freak, but you show me anyone who runs their own business who isn't.'

'I'm not sure I could. Are sales doing okay?' I ask as we are now walking along.

'Yeah. In fact, sales have been brilliant these past few days. My daughter is really good – being a hair and make-up business is something she is really interested in.'

'I can understand how losing your last job would make you feel a bit insecure about an income, but it sounds like your daughter is doing just fine. You're no use to anyone if you're completely burned out, are you?'

He turns to me and smiles. 'You're right. That's what my mum says.'

I'm not sure how I feel about sounding like someone's mother.

'So, I made a vow to only check in on the website once, late in the evening.'

'And are you sticking to it?'

'Yep. I've been out swimming, walking and jet-skiing, completely freeing my mind. I even discovered an early morning yoga session on a beach back on Kos, which I wish I'd known about sooner.'

'I used to go there. It's a wonder we never ran into each other.'

'I know, although I only discovered it yesterday when I was out on an early morning run. Anyway, when I do check the website in the evening,' he says, returning to talk of his business, 'sales are doing so well that I've allowed myself to switch off a little.'

'Glad to hear it. That has to be doing you good.'

We've begun to walk a little downhill, and when we reach a bench, we both sit down.

'Fancy an ice cream?' says Dean, gesturing to a shop nearby with an ice-cream stand outside.

'Go on then.'

A few minutes later, we're enjoying cooling ice creams and enjoying the view of the vista below, of rolling hills and a view of the sea beyond.

'Ah this is nice,' says Dean, soaking up the pretty surroundings. 'Cheers.' He taps his ice-cream cornet next to mine, which makes me smile. 'Actually, shall we do a "cheers" with a proper drink tonight?' he asks and I find myself keen to accept. Dean is delightful company, a real force of nature who is engaging and funny.

'Sure, why not,' I reply.

'Great. Maybe you can recommend somewhere to eat as you've been here a day or two already?'

'Actually, I can.' I think of the restaurant I dined at last night with the rooftop terrace that was not far from here and had a beautiful view.

'That is, unless you prefer to be down at the port in Skala, where it's a little busier?' I suggest.

'No, around here is fine, I don't want to be staggering up the hill after a few beers.' He laughs.

It turns out Dean is renting a room just around the corner from where I'm staying, so I agree to meet him at this very bench at seven thirty for dinner.

'So, what brings you here to Patmos?' I ask him.

'The room I found is incredibly cheap, so I thought I'd do a little exploring here for two nights. I read about the holy cave, so thought I'd visit.'

'Are you religious then?'

'Not really, if I'm honest, but my gran isn't too well at the moment, so I thought I'd light a candle and say a bit of a prayer. I wouldn't normally do that kind of thing but, well, it's a holy place, isn't it? So it can't do any harm.'

I'm not sure that's how it works if you're not a true believer, but I don't tell him that.

'Well, I think that's a lovely thing to do. I'm sure she'll be thrilled that you went to the trouble.'

'Oh, I won't tell her.' He frowns. 'She'll think she's on her bloody last legs if I say I've been praying for her.' He laughs loudly and I find myself laughing too.

We chat for a little while longer, then Dean glances at his

watch. 'I should be going if I want to visit the cave before it clos-es,' he says, finishing his ice cream. 'See you later then.'

He heads off, leaving the scent of his citrusy aftershave in his wake. Dean clearly likes the good things in life, judging by his expensive haircut, veneered teeth and designer sunglasses. Not to mention the Rolex he spent twisting around his wrist during take-off. He kind of screams money, despite revealing that he has only just started the new internet business, so is obviously a guy who believes image is everything.

I can't deny that, even though he is never the kind of guy I would ever be attracted to, he has a very endearing personality and would make a good holiday buddy. I kind of wish I'd met up with him in Kos. I could imagine him having a lot of fun with us all when we'd spent the evenings at Mambo's, or going through our stretches at Theo's yoga classes on the beach.

I find myself walking on with a smile across my face thinking of what easy company Dean is, and how he seems a world away from the nervous traveller I encountered on the plane, twiddling with the strap on his wristwatch. I slightly regret my initial caution towards him when we first met on the plane, but I think maybe I didn't feel as strong as I usually do after me being ill. It left me feeling a little exposed and vulnerable.

There is no doubt that being in the sunshine has done me the world of good, this past week or so, and I feel better than I have done in a long time, ready to take on the world.

TWENTY-SIX

I fling the patio doors open and sit on the sofa in my bathrobe, really enjoying the sound of the music pounding in my ears, thinking how earbuds are the greatest invention ever as you don't disturb the neighbours. I'm so engrossed in my music that I don't hear my telephone ringing inside my straw bag.

I pick a knee-length white dress and some red canvas espadrilles that I match with the jaunty red straw hat I bought down at Skala today, and a slash of red lipstick instead of my usual pink.

I arrive at the agreed bench, where I met Dean earlier, at half past seven precisely but Dean is nowhere to be seen, so I take a seat and wait. A couple of minutes later, I hear the sound of a slow wolf whistle as he appears from around a corner.

'Sorry, I bet men are not even allowed to do that these days, are they?' He laughs.

'Probably not,' I agree.

'At least it's still okay to pay a woman a compliment, so I will. You look gorgeous.'

'Why, thank you. You scrub up pretty well too.'

He's dressed in a pair of tight navy jeans, which are probably designer, and a busy-patterned blue shirt, which is definitely designer, the Calvin Klein logo being a bit of a giveaway.

'Cheers. Are you hungry? I'm starved,' he says as I push up from the bench and we walk along together towards the restaurant.

'Did you light a candle for your gran then?' I ask as we stroll.

'I did. Although she will probably be around for a long time yet. She's been living with bowel cancer for the past three years.'

'I'm so sorry to hear that.'

'Thanks. But honestly, she just gets on with life, she's never without a smile. She was told by doctors that she might have six months after her diagnosis but she was adamant they were wrong. She said she wanted to see her granddaughter, my niece, start school before she went anywhere, and it looks like she will. Katy starts school in September.'

'She sounds like an amazing woman,' I say, thinking of how the human spirit never ceases to amaze me.

We arrive at the restaurant and climb the stairs to the seating area on the terrace, where we are shown to a table.

'Great choice. Look at that view,' says Dean, casting his eyes over the view below of the hillsides and sea.

'When are you going home?' Dean asks, after we've ordered a drink, deciding to share a bottle of wine.

'I'm not exactly sure,' I tell him.

'I got the impression you were a bit of a free spirit.' He smiles. 'You give off that kind of vibe. In fact, I'm surprised you chose a touristy place like Kos. I thought you'd be hanging out on a beach in Ibiza.'

'Isn't that a bit of a stereotype?' I take a sip of crisp white wine that the waiter has just placed on the table. 'Thinking Ibiza is full of artists and hippies. Of which I am neither, by the way.'

'I just meant the quieter places in Ibiza where people live all year round. The creative types, not the holidaymakers who get off their face in the nightclubs. I suppose this place has more of a relaxed vibe though. Is that why you came here?'

'Hmm, maybe, but there's a bit more to it than that,' I find myself saying.

'Go on then,' he says as he pours us another glass of wine.

'Go on what?'

'Tell me the story of why you're here, if there's more to it than being a tourist. I think I practically told you my life story on the flight over, didn't I?' He laughs and I recall he did, chatting away in an attempt to calm his nerves on the flight.

I take a deep breath and find myself telling Dean all about the letter I found and how my sister lives here on the island. He's so easy to talk to.

'That's amazing,' he says with his usual positivity.

'Is it?'

'Of course it is. You're both still young, you have years to get to know each other.' He beams and I could kiss him. He's definitely a glass half-full kind of bloke. Just the sort of person I needed, and I feel a weight has been lifted a little.

'So, you're doing this alone then, no bloke with you?' he asks, perusing the menu, and I wonder whether he fancies me.

'Nope. Let's just say, I'm happily single at the moment,' I tell him, even though I kind of wish Georgios had been in contact.

'Me, too. Cheers to being young, free and single, hey?' He lifts his wine glass, and we clink them together. 'At least I think I am?' He laughs.

'Which bit, young or single?'

'Single. I'm kind of seeing someone, but it's not really going anywhere. Besides, I don't have a lot of spare money while the business is building, and it's not fair to never have the money to go out together.'

'Yet here you are on holiday?' I can't help commenting.

'Ah, but I never exactly paid for it. My dad could see I was almost burned out, so he put some money in my account whilst the business is still building up and told me to take a break. In fact, he insisted.'

'So you were forced into taking a holiday?' I can't help smiling.

'Yeah. It sounds weird when you put it like that, doesn't it. My parents have always had my best interests at heart though. My dad had a heart attack two years ago, a mild one thankfully, but I think he was worried I might be heading the same way.'

We dine on delicious lamb *kleftico*, which I haven't eaten since I've been here, and I enjoy every tasty mouthful. Dean has me laughing throughout the meal, telling me stories about himself and friends, and the things they get up to together. At the end of the meal, Dean tries to pay, which feels completely wrong, as we are just two new friends having dinner together. And his financial situation isn't exactly rosy right now.

'Let me get this one,' I insist. 'I've had such a great time. And you're a really good listener, thank you.'

After much protesting, I settle the bill and we walk out onto the street once more. Dean stops in front of one of the bars on the way home.

'At least let me buy you another drink then. Maybe a cocktail. I still feel bad that you paid for dinner.'

'How do you know I'm not a secret millionaire?' I tease and he just laughs. 'Sure, why not? A cocktail sounds lovely, thanks, and a mojito just happens to be my favourite.'

We find a table that has just been vacated outside the bar and Dean orders two mojitos. It feels so lovely sitting here with such engaging company, and the evening has distracted me from thinking about Georgios. Until now that is. Sitting here down the quiet backstreet watching the orange sunset, I find he enters my thoughts once more.

Finishing our drinks, Dean walks me home and as we head back, I get the feeling someone is following us. I think it might be my neighbours, walking home from an evening out, but when I turn around, no one is there.

At my apartment, Dean thanks me once again for the meal.

'You're very welcome. I'm glad I ran into you again.'

'I'll be off walking in the hills tomorrow, then I'm taking a ferry back to Kos in the late afternoon. So, I might not see you again. You take care of yourself.'

'You too, Dean.' We embrace each other as a brother and sister might.

'And good luck with your sister, I'm sure it will all work out,' he says kindly.

'I hope so.'

'It will. Just go and knock on the door. What is it they say? Face your fear and do it anyway. Oh, and don't forget to check out the website,' he reminds me. 'If you ever fancy a new look with hair extensions.'

'You never know. I do like to change things up a bit.'

'Tell your sister too. Spread the word in Greece. We ship international.' He winks. 'See you, Orla.'

'Bye, Dean. Good luck with everything.'

'You too.'

Once inside, I flop down onto the sofa, and open my bag and glance at my phone to discover I have had a missed call. The time shows it was earlier this afternoon and I realise it must have been when I had my headphones in listening to music.

I check my voicemail for messages, and my pulse rate quickens when I hear the voice of Georgios, simply saying he would try to ring another time. It's just after eleven o'clock, and I wonder whether or not it's too late to call him back. Why would Georgios call me, I wonder? He chose to say goodbye the evening of the BBQ and he hadn't even asked me for my number, so obviously he got it from Sophia. I thought there was little else to say. I can't help feeling a little bit excited that he's called though, and decide to call him back.

I can feel my heart racing as the phone rings out, expecting to hear his voice at any moment but it goes to voicemail and my heart sinks. I wonder what to say when the bleep of the answerphone flicks on, and find myself simply saying I am returning his call. When I hang up, I regret not saying how nice it was to hear from him but there's nothing I can do about that now.

Lying on the bed, I think of the wonderful time I spent with Georgios over on Kos, particularly the day we visited the ruins of Aghios Stefanos, after he'd picked me up in his speedboat. I recall the walk along the beach in the dark after he'd taken me to the restaurant near the sea. But most of all, I think of how I spilled my innermost secret to him. Something I had never told anyone else. They say it's good to unburden yourself to a stranger, knowing you will never see them again, yet I yearn to see Georgios and just maybe he wants to see me again too.

Feeling restless, I make myself a cup of peppermint tea, and take it outside to drink beneath the stars. I toy with the idea of leaving another voicemail, but decide against it. Instead, I read a few chapters of my new book but find I can't really concentrate. Eventually I head to bed, wondering if I will ever hear from Georgios again.

TWENTY-SEVEN

The next morning, I rise early and take a walk, enjoying the almost silence of my surroundings. I watch the sunrise from behind the mountains, recalling the wonderful yoga sessions on the beach at Kos as I head downhill, passing elderly residents who greet me with a nod or a smile and I say *kalimera* to them.

An hour later, as I'm returning to my apartment, I pass a house with two little girls sitting in a doorway playing with their dolls. The cute sisters look around a year apart in age; the older-looking one picks up a brush and combs the doll's long blonde hair, in contrast to the children's dark, silky locks. A pang of regret engulfs me once more as I think of the years growing up without a sister and how I would have dearly loved one, but it wasn't to be.

I pop into a shop and buy some fresh orange juice, thinking I might take breakfast on the terrace this morning and walk home feeling inspired by a day filled with possibilities and trying hard to bury thoughts of Georgios.

I'm not going to put it off any longer. Today, I'm going to visit the address on the envelope, after I've written a letter to post through the door, in case there is no one at home. I've also decided to stay on in Patmos for a few more days.

As I approach my door, my phone rings. To my astonishment it is Georgios.

'Did the cave live up to your expectations then?' he asks.

'Georgios. Hi.' My heart is hammering in my chest at the sound of his voice. I can't believe he is calling me.

'Yes, it did. I found it very moving. How did you get my number?' I ask, thrilled to hear his voice.

'From your friend Chloe. I did ask Sophia, but she said something about confidentiality of guests. So, are you enjoying Patmos?' he asks.

'It's really lovely.' I try to keep my voice upbeat, hiding the disappointment I felt at him not being around to say goodbye on the morning I left. 'It's very quiet and rugged here, probably the ideal place to write a novel.'

'Perhaps I should have spent some time there then. Maybe I still will,' he says, and my heart leaps at the thought of him coming over here.

'It would be lovely to see you,' I say, before kicking myself. He never said that he would like to see me, but simply that he might visit the island.

'That's good to know.' He pauses for a moment. 'Have you made contact with your sister yet?'

'No, I haven't. To be honest, I've been putting it off a little, filling my days with sightseeing and chatting to people.'

'Well, I'm sure you will do it when you're ready. It's a big thing to confront.'

I can't help thinking how his measured response is in complete contrast to Dean's.

'So, have you met any interesting people?' Georgios asks and for some reason, I don't immediately tell him about Dean.

'One or two, yes. I have some lovely neighbours here.' I wonder why I didn't mention Dean and feel slightly annoyed with myself. We were nothing more than friends, and Georgios has certainly never indicated that he wanted more from us. There's a pause in our conversation for a few seconds before he speaks again.

'So, are you free for dinner this evening? Unless you are dining with your gentleman friend again?'

'What?' I can feel my cheeks burning. How on earth would he know about that?

'You mean Dean? He was a guy I met on the plane coming over. I bumped into him here.' I really wish I had mentioned him now. 'Have you been spying on me or something?' I'm completely confused.

'Not exactly spying, just observing,' he says. 'Anyway, stop talking and turn around,' he instructs.

I turn around and as I glance down the hill, I can barely believe my eyes as Georgios is slowly walking towards me. He looks every bit as gorgeous as I remember as he stands in front of me.

'Hi, Orla, it's good to see you.'

'Oh my goodness, I can't believe you are actually here. It's good to see you.'

'It's good to see you too.' He smiles at me, and steps forward as though he is about to embrace me in a hug, but I turn to open the front door. Annoyingly, as I turn to let us inside, his presence makes me fumble so much, I drop my key on the floor.

'Here, let me.' He takes the key from me, an electric charge passing between us as our fingers collide. Suddenly I'm in his arms and he's kissing me with a passion he has never kissed me with before, and my insides turn to jelly.

'Shall we go inside? Unless you want your new neighbours gossiping about you,' he says, locking eyes with me.

'What made you decide to come here, now?' I ask, once we're inside, trying to keep my cool and completely failing. I try and keep my voice upbeat, hiding the disappointment I felt at him not saying goodbye, especially after we shared that lovely kiss. I wonder what he is doing here, now. 'I wasn't sure I would see you again,' I say, determined not to be so easily seduced.

'I never doubted I would see you again,' he replies.

My head is whirring with so many questions that I want to ask him, but as he steps closer to me, I can feel my resolve weakening. It seems Georgios isn't in the mood for talking right now, and if I'm completely honest with myself, he isn't the only one. When he kisses me again and leads me towards the bedroom, I don't resist.

'Georgios, where is this going?' I ask, somehow unable to tear myself away from him, as he starts to unbutton my dress.

'Wherever you want it to,' he answers, breathlessly.

I consider that maybe the time for talking can wait just a little while longer...

Later, we're sat enjoying a beer on the balcony, my head still spinning from what has just happened between us.

'I still can't believe you're actually here,' I tell him yet again and he smiles.

'I hope it was a pleasant surprise. I always intended to come here,' he tells me.

'When did you arrive in Patmos?' I ask, realising he'd mentioned seeing me with Dean last night.

'Yesterday afternoon. I called you but there was no answer, so I wasn't even sure if you were still on Patmos. That evening, I ate at a local café bar and when I left, I saw you walking along with another man.' He sips his beer.

'So, you were following me?' I recall the feeling of someone walking behind Dean and I last night.

'Not exactly, but I didn't know who the guy you were with was, or what your plans were for the rest of the evening. I wasn't certain I would be given a warm welcome, so I left you to it, deciding to contact you today instead,' he explains.

'Well, if you had hung around for a little longer, you would have noticed me going into my apartment. Alone.'

'I'm sorry, Orla.' He sighs. 'For not being around when you left. I regret that now.' He speaks softly.

'I'm sorry too,' I reply. 'I enjoyed the time we spent together and I thought the feeling was mutual.' I try hard to keep the emotion from my voice. 'I kept thinking of how I'd confided in you. I haven't even told Polly about my sister, and she's my best friend.'

'Of course I enjoyed spending time with you, Orla, surely you knew that? And I feel honoured that I am the person you shared your secret with.' He reaches across the table and takes my hand in his, kissing it gently. 'But I was under pressure to complete the book, which I have finished by the way. I needed to fully concentrate, but then along came a very pleasant distraction. I'm sorry if I gave you mixed messages,' he says softly.

'I guess you did. I won't lie, I was left feeling completely confused.'

'You weren't the only one who was confused. I got the impression you wanted nothing more than to travel, like a wild, free bird that doesn't want to be caged. Can you blame me for feeling a little conflicted?'

'No, I suppose not.' I realise his words have truth in them as I think of how I told Georgios of my desire to spend every second of my life exploring the world and how I grow bored easily, so perhaps he was just trying to protect his own feelings.

'I still can't believe you're here,' I say, staring at his beautiful face opposite me on the balcony in the bright sunshine.

'Well, I am. And I intend to make sure we enjoy every minute of our time together.' He leans across the table and kisses me softly on the lips. 'But today, I think there is something that you finally need to confront. It's the main reason you came to Patmos, after all.'

'I know. But now you are here I can do it tomorrow...'

'Do it today,' he says gently. 'Would you like me to come with you?' he adds.

'Maybe. Even if it's to make sure I don't turn around and run away.'

Georgios nips inside for a quick shower, leaving me with my thoughts swirling as I experience a mixture of delight yet uncertainty. I really thought I had seen the last of Georgios, and yet he has walked back into my life and I wonder where this is all heading. He has been on my mind since I left Kos and now it's clear he had been thinking about me too. I'm looking forward to dinner tonight, trying to take one day at a time; after all, that's what I always do.

I text Polly to see if she is free, feeling the need to talk things over with her. A few minutes later, she calls.

'Hey, my friend, how's things in sunny Greece?' she asks.

'Oh, it's lovely. How are things with you?'

'Good, thanks. I'm just having a coffee after work in Costa before I go shopping, so good timing.'

'Are you alone?'

'Completely. So, what have you been up to?' she asks brightly.

I find myself pouring my heart out about Georgios, and she listens without interrupting me.

'Wow,' she says finally. 'A moody writer, who just happens to be gorgeous. You always meet the most interesting people. And he's followed you over to Patmos! Oh, my goodness, he must be keen.'

'I know. Oh, Polly, he seems to have really got under my skin, which is exactly what I didn't want, or need right now.' I sigh.

'Why not?'

'I'm not sure. Sometimes I think I am better off being alone.'

Or maybe this time, I don't want to risk heartache.

'You're too hard on yourself. You've been through a lot lately, so maybe you should just see where life takes you, and I don't just mean geographically.' She laughs. 'Take a chance, life is far too short as you are forever telling other people,' she reminds me.

'I guess you're right. Thanks, Polly, it's always good to talk to you.'

We chat a while longer, before I tell her I am going for dinner with Georgios this evening.

'Well, have a great time,' she says. 'He sounds like a very interesting bloke. And I'd say you've gotten under his skin too. He's travelled over to another island to see you, after all. Just have fun.'

'Thanks, Polly, I will.'

'Right, I probably need to get going now. I'm shopping for a new top. I'm out tonight too, with Tim. We're going for a meal and then to the cinema.'

'Enjoy yourself. I'm really happy things are going well between you and Tim; you are absolutely my favourite couple.'

'Ah, thanks, Orla. Speak to you soon. Enjoy yourself.'

I think about Polly's wise words as I wait for Georgios. Perhaps she's right, I shouldn't be so afraid of relationships. What will be will be. I rifle through my wardrobe to select something to wear for what I hope will be a romantic dinner later. I also feel guilty that I haven't told my best friend about the other reason I am here in Patmos. But maybe it's best until I actually find out how things are going to turn out first.

After I shower and change, I persuade Georgios to join me in a drive. We drive uphill towards the huge monastery that towers over the streets, before heading down across the other side of the small island. Parking, we follow a footpath that will eventually lead down towards the harbour at Skala. A church bell rings out from a small white church on the hillside, and to my delight a wedding is taking place. We hang back and watch the beautiful bride and groom and their families emerge from the church. They look so happy and I hope their love lasts forever.

'What an absolutely gorgeous place for a wedding,' I comment and Georgios agrees.

'Probably less chance of rain here, although they do say it's good luck if it rains on your wedding day,' Georgios tells me, but I can't imagine why.

Georgios takes my hand as we make our way along a slightly overgrown path. A few olive trees are dotted along the path and, in the distance, a couple of goats are grazing in the garden of a crumbling farmhouse. There aren't many farms here on an industrial scale, as most of the island earns its income from tourism, but local residents still keep goats and grow vegetables in their gardens. Soon we pass through a forest that has newly planted trees.

'This must be the area where the new saplings have been planted. Over two thousand, I believe. I heard about this on the news,' Georgios tells me. 'The previous trees were destroyed by a pest apparently. The path leads to the Apocalypse cave, so the islanders were keen to re-plant the forest.'

'Interesting. I guess they have to keep the area looking attractive as the island relies so heavily on tourism.'

'Talking of tourists, have you decided where you are going next?' Georgios asks as we walk along in the bright sunshine.

'I've been thinking about that. If I get a warm reception from my sister, I might stay here on Patmos for a while longer. I'd like to visit Samos though. It looks really pretty.'

After sharing everything I was feeling for Georgios and fully resolving to meet my sister, I don't feel the urgency to be heading off on a new adventure. Right now, everything seems to be going pretty well right here.

'It is. I haven't been for many years, but from what I recall it's a very pretty island. They produce a delicious sweet muscat wine. It's also the birthplace of Pythagoras,' he tells me knowledgeably. 'Have you planned any further than that?'

I think of back home, Dad, Polly, and my friends. I have so much to tell them, so I should make my way back some time soon. I hope my sister will feel comfortable enough to come and visit. I think it would be nice for Dad if my sister and I became friends. I don't want Dad to think it is something I can't forgive him for, as he couldn't be more wrong.

'Not really. I will definitely be flying home from Rhodes at some point though. I can't stay in Greece forever.'

'I'll probably be going home soon too,' he says. 'Although I guess I could stay here in Greece if I wanted to; I can write my novels from anywhere in the world. But there's always something that pulls me back to England.'

'Unpredictable weather? Traffic jams?'

'I know, it seems crazy.' He laughs. 'Especially when we are surrounded by this.' He glances around at the breathtaking view. 'But I like London, as much as I like Greece. I suppose I like the contrast of the two places. It's also where my publisher is.'

Soon enough we are back near my rented accommodation and sitting at a café overlooking the sea, sipping an ice-cold beer.

'Are you ready then?'

Georgios reaches across the table and takes my hand.

'Ready.' I take a deep breath and try and quell the rising nerves in my stomach.

We walk along silently until we reach the little row of rough stone white houses. Georgios asks me if I want him to stay, but we agree on him returning to the apartment to wait to hear from me.

I glance at the little red front door, slightly ajar, when suddenly a black cat emerges from it and crosses my path. Is that supposed to be good luck or bad? I can't remember.

I walk as slowly as a bride in a church on her wedding day as I approach the house. It's now or never. I'm about to knock on the door, when it opens and a young woman stands before me. I gasp at the sight of the dark-haired woman, who, apart from her colouring, looks exactly like me. She even has the same dark-grey eyes. She runs her eyes all over my face, frowning at first, then smiling and crying as her hand flies to her mouth, somehow knowing I am her sister before I even say a word. I take the letter from my bag and she invites me inside.

Her English is very good, although not perfect.

'My father's daughter,' she repeats. 'My sister. I have a sister,' she utters, gripping my hand in hers.

We have both dried our eyes from our happy tears and are drinking tea in the rear garden of the house. I learn she is a teacher in a primary school and she shares the house with her friend, who works at the monastery.

I explain how my mother was gravely ill when her letter arrived, which is probably why she never had a response.

'It does not matter.' She shakes her head. 'You are here now. Do you think my father would like to meet me?'

'*Our* father,' I remind her, and she smiles. 'And I'm sure he would. Especially when he realises how happy I am to have discovered you. Let me give him a call.'

So, on that sunny day in my sister Sula's garden in Patmos, I call Dad. I can hear his intake of breath, when I tell him how I discovered the letter and how I tracked her down. I ask if he would like to do a video phone call and he makes a joke about going to change his shirt first as he's gardening, no doubt needing time to gather his thoughts. He calls a short while later, and sees his other daughter for the very first time. There are tears, but also laughter and Dad tells Sula he would love to meet her for real.

Sula and I agree to meet for dinner tomorrow night, as she has something on this evening. I walk home to tell Georgios, almost floating on air.

TWENTY-EIGHT

Later that evening, Georgios takes me to an intimate restaurant that he stumbled upon when he arrived here last night. It's down a backstreet, and has bunting stretched across the narrow street; the restaurant has stone-coloured walls, and is squeezed in between a bar and an ice-cream shop.

'This is nice.' I glance across the table at him on an outside terrace the flickering flame of a candle between us.

'It's pretty special. I got talking to someone last night, and they recommended this place. I took the liberty of booking a table.'

'It's a good job you did.' I glance inside the bustling restaurant, waiters darting about delivering tasty-looking dishes to diners. The interior walls are white, the tables and chairs black, covered with thick white cotton tablecloths. The glasses are crystal, and the silver heavy and expensive looking. Outside here on the terrace, there are beautiful flowers in pots and a water feature in the corner; a string of white lights are threaded through the trees above. I can't help thinking it will cost an arm and a leg to dine here.

A waiter arrives and pours a glass of red wine for us to try, and it tastes wonderful.

'You look beautiful tonight,' says Georgios.

'Thank you.'

'I'm so glad I came here,' he says as he looks into my eyes, reaching his hand across the table to mine. 'And I'm so happy things went well with your sister. I can't wait to meet her. Assuming you want me to,' he quickly adds.

'Of course I do,' I say, really meaning it.

'And if you want some company, maybe I could join you in Samos for a couple of days?' he offers.

'Really?' I feel thrilled at the thought of wandering the streets of Samos hand in hand with Georgios and having long, lazy lie-ins together.

'I'd like nothing more,' I tell him.

'Great. Let's check out the ferry crossings later.' He smiles.

We dine on fabulous food, all served beautifully and I feel as though I might be in a Michelin-star restaurant somewhere, rather than a backstreet restaurant in a Greek village. Georgios chooses tender lamb in a redcurrant sauce, and I have chicken in a delightful rosemary cream sauce, with root vegetables and oven-roasted potatoes.

'I don't think I'll ever forget this.' I glance down at the twinkling lights of the houses in the valley below. 'It's just perfect.'

'It is.' He follows my gaze. 'Although I hope this is only the start of our adventure. Maybe you could come to London for a weekend, when we get back to England. I could come and see you in Cheshire, too?'

'I'd like that. Coming to London, I mean. I've actually never been before.'

'Really? Then we need to do something about that,' says Georgios. 'I would love to show you around.'

'I'd like that. I'm not sure why I haven't visited London. I guess I've been too busy travelling to places abroad than exploring places in England, I suppose.'

'Sometimes we don't always appreciate what we have under our nose,' he says, gazing at me.

Later, as we walk the cobbled streets back to my apartment, I feel like I could burst with happiness. Especially when Georgios takes my hand and leads me down an alley, where he presses me against a wall and kisses me. A plate clatters in a nearby house somewhere followed by the bark of a dog, so we giggle and move on like a couple of teenagers who are about to be caught in the act. Walking home beneath the light of the moon, I know this is an evening I will remember for a very long time to come.

The following evening with Sula was wonderful as well. We laughed throughout the meal, discovering we enjoyed the same sense of humour. She brought along her housemate, Luisa, maybe in case the evening was a little awkward, but it was nothing of the sort. Georgios came too and the four of us talked and laughed until the early hours.

We spent the next two days getting to know Sula, and I discovered she is a talented painter, her house displaying several watercolours of the harbour. I think of how I enjoy drawing too, although I would concede that Sula has far more talent. I can't wait to get to know her more, and she has already booked her plane ticket to visit us in England in a couple of weeks' time.

The sun burns down onto the deck of the ferry as we make our way to Samos, the huge monastery on Patmos slowly disappearing out of sight. I'm curled up on a bench, leaning against Georgios and reading as he stares out across the open sea.

The boat is packed with tourists, who are snapping away with their cameras as we approach Samos, the white houses with the red roofs beckoning us towards them.

'Are you thinking about your next book?' I ask, placing down the book I am reading and sitting up.

'Perhaps I should be, but truthfully, I don't want to think about books for a while, at least not writing one.'

'Do you read much in your leisure time?'

'Only on holiday. Science fiction, usually,' he reveals.

'I can imagine that's a real antidote to the stuff you write about.'

'Exactly.' He laughs, extending his arm for me to cuddle into again. We both stare out across the clear blue water, looking forward to spending the next few days wandering the streets of Samos.

'Anyway, talking of books, I'm pleased my own is finished. And thankfully, the ending turned out exactly as I hoped it would. I didn't want to have to change it.' He looks at me and grins.

'What do you mean, it turned out as you hoped it would? Surely there can be no doubt how the story ends, as you are the author?'

'Usually. But this time, I was never really sure where the story was heading,' he reveals.

'How do you mean?' I sit up.

'I wasn't certain that the two main characters would fall in love. They seemed so different. I didn't think it could ever work. In the end though, it appears that they weren't quite so different after all.'

'Really? How were they similar?' This has me intrigued now.

'Well, they both enjoyed travelling, never really wanting to commit to love. The male love interest had been hurt, believing he had been in love, but it turns out he never was. Not when he compared it to how he felt about the heroine in the story. The main difference between them was that the male confronted things and was usually outspoken, whereas the heroine tended to avoid confrontation. I was never quite sure how the story would conclude.'

It takes me a minute to take in what Georgios has just said.

'You wrote about us?' I am absolutely speechless.

'Not originally, but my love story was going nowhere. I just wasn't feeling it, as you know. Then one day you made a comment about truth being stranger than fiction. As I got to know you, I decided to write about us. Every meeting was another chapter in our story.'

'You've written the story of us?' My heart is almost bursting with love.

'Well, the story so far. So, you see, I had to come to Patmos to discover the ending of the book. Maybe we will have a real-life happy ending too.'

I wrap my arms around him and kiss him, and I don't care who is watching.

'You really are a very surprising man, infuriating at times, but surprising.'

'I'm glad you think so. I wouldn't want you growing bored, given your penchant for changing your mind,' he says, before we kiss again.

'I don't think there's any danger of that. At least not for a long time.'

The ship's horn sounds then, signalling our arrival at Samos Harbour.

'I'm glad to hear it,' he says as we prepare for our next adventure. This time, together.

EPILOGUE

'So, are we flying back to London or Manchester?' Georgios asked me one evening, after three gorgeous days in Samos, as we lounged around the pool of the hotel and talked about booking flights home.

I'd had the most wonderful time with Georgios, trying sweet muscat wine after dinner and finding secluded spots for picnics on a quad bike, and it was ending far too soon. But just because it was time for us to return to England didn't mean I was leaving anything behind...

'Maybe Manchester? I want to see Dad and make sure he's okay before I come and see you in London,' I told him. 'And I'd like you to meet him, if it's not too soon?' I said, and he'd smiled and said he would love to meet my dad.

'You place is lovely. Exactly as I imagined it somehow,' said Georgios when he walked through the door of my first-floor apartment. I placed my green felt hat on the old-fashioned coat stand in the hallway and led Georgios into the cosy lounge, bright with cushions, plants and colourful paintings on the soft-grey walls.

Dad and Georgios got along like a house on fire when they first met, then I travelled to London for a while to be with Georgios, while counting down the days until Sula would visit.

When she arrived, we took Dad to his favourite pub for Sunday lunch.

As we sat together for the first time, Dad kept glancing between me and Sula, pride written across his face, despite the circumstances. I was so pleased that all three of us had been getting on so well. I knew she would be a part of our lives forever.

One afternoon during Sula's visit, I took her to the Greasy Spoon to meet Polly and we had a lovely afternoon, heading into town afterwards to do some shopping.

'Polly, I'm so sorry I never said anything to you before now,' I said the following day and she gripped my hand and told me not to be silly. 'I just wanted to meet her first, and see how things went.'

'Of course you did. And she's lovely.'

I was later to learn from Dad that he had met Sula's mother in Greece, when she had stayed at Maria's hotel one year, explaining that he and Mum had been having problems at the time. He told me honestly, that maybe it had been an infatuation, a midlife crisis even, but guilt got the better of him and he returned home, unaware she was pregnant with his child. Thankfully, he and Mum made up and I honestly think they were happy until the day she died.

'See you soon, sis,' I said when Sula caught a flight back to Greece. It was hard saying goodbye, but we're making up for lost time and it's wonderful. We Skype regularly and I've already booked a flight for a long weekend next month, where Sula is meeting me in Kos.

I headed off to London to stay with Georgios, for the second time in a month. I've decided to rent out my apartment to someone at Potters – after I decided to do the sensible thing and buy it – as Dad's perfectly happy for me to spend time with him when I return from my travels. And, of course, Sula is welcome over any time.

'So, how's it going?' Georgios places a coffee down at the side of the computer in his spacious London flat, where I am working away.

'Amazing! I've had such lovely comments from readers,' I tell him excitedly.

I decided to write a travel blog, uploading pictures and stories of my travels, and more recently our travels and it's had a great response from viewers. And, of course, Georgios' writing tips have been invaluable. Readers have loved reading of our romantic journey, and Georgios has even seen a surge in sales of his last book, which of course I talk about in my blog, with a link to buy.

'I'm proud of you,' he says, dropping a kiss on my head.

'What for?' I stand up and lean into him, enjoying a lingering hug.

'For figuring out what you want to do in life. And for not running away from finding your sister.'

'I almost did. I'm glad you were there that day.'

'Oh, and by the way, I think you are a natural writer.'

'Maybe not natural but I have a great teacher,' I reply modestly.

'Well, that's true, I suppose.' He adopts a serious expression. 'I should be charging you by the hour really. By the way, have you written anything about Paris?' he asks.

'I haven't, I didn't really take any photos when I went there. Why do you ask?'

'A piece about the Moulin Rouge might be interesting.'

'Ooh, it would be. I kind of wish I'd gone there now,' I say, recalling how I never had the courage to watch the show alone.

Georgios goes to a drawer and takes out a folder containing tickets for a trip to Paris, taking in a show at the Moulin Rouge.

'Oh my goodness, Georgios! This is amazing! When do we leave?' I ask excitedly.

'Tomorrow afternoon. If that's alright with you?'

'Of course it's alright. It's more than alright. It's fabulous. I can't believe you remembered me telling you about that.'

'I remember everything you ever told me.'

I crush him in an embrace, thinking I might just be the luckiest woman in the whole world.

A LETTER FROM SUE

Dear reader,

I want to say a huge thank you for choosing to read *Take a Chance on Greece*. If you did enjoy it, and want to keep up to date with all my latest releases, just sign up at the following link. Your email address will never be shared and you can unsubscribe at any time.

www.bookouture.com/sue-roberts

I really hope you loved *Take a Chance on Greece* and if you did, I would be very grateful if you could write a review. I'd love to hear what you think, and it makes such a difference helping new readers to discover one of my books for the first time. I guess we've all had dreams of taking off and living somewhere sunny, and stories such as *Take a Chance on Greece* might even inspire us!

I love hearing from my readers – you can get in touch on my Facebook page, through Twitter, Goodreads or my website. Thank you all so much.

Thanks,

Sue Roberts

KEEP IN TOUCH WITH SUE

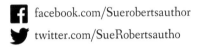

facebook.com/Suerobertsauthor

twitter.com/SueRobertsautho

ACKNOWLEDGEMENTS

I would like to say a huge thanks to Emily Gowers and Natalie Edwards for their wonderful work on this book. Once again, it goes without saying how grateful I am to every single person that makes up the fabulous publisher that is Bookouture. Kim, Noelle, Sarah and Jess work tirelessly to introduce our books to new audiences, and I know this book couldn't be in better hands!

And, of course, thank you so much to every single reader who has bought one of my books and sent me lovely messages. Big shout out to book bloggers for their advance reviews and positive comments. I am truly grateful to you all.

Printed in Great Britain
by Amazon